ONE WAY TICKET

D1297626

One way ticket
Migration and female labour

Edited by

Annie Phizacklea

Routledge & Kegan Paul
London, Boston, Melbourne and Henley

First published in 1983
by Routledge & Kegan Paul plc
39 Store Street, London WC1E 7DD,
9 Park Street, Boston, Mass. 02108, USA,
296 Beaconsfield Parade, Middle Park,
Melbourne, 3206, Australia, and
Broadway House, Newtown Road,
Henley-on-Thames, Oxon RG9 1EN
Printed in Great Britain by
T.J. Press Ltd, Padstow, Cornwall
© Routledge & Kegan Paul plc

Library of Congress Cataloging in Publication Data

One way ticket.
Bibliography: p.
Includes index.
1. Alien labor--Europe--Addresses, essays, lectures.
2. Women--Employment--Europe--Addresses, essays, lectures.
3. Discrimination in employment--Europe--Addresses, essays,
lectures.   I. Phizacklea, Annie.
HD8378.5.A2052 1983   331.4'12791   83-3092

ISBN 0-7100-9489-2

Contents

v

Acknowledgments

My greatest thanks go to each of the contributors whose hard work, friendship and support made the book possible.

I am also indebted to the Social Science Research Council for paying me a salary for the initial period of research on this project and later, in conjunction with the Centre National de la Recherche Scientifique, for awarding me a grant to carry out research in France.

There are a number of individuals who have read and commented on various parts of this manuscript - Stephen Castles, Caroline Freeman, Denis Kandiyoti, Alison Lever and Jackie West - my sincerest thanks to each of you.

I am particularly grateful to Nancy Lineton for typing the manuscript so well and to Philippa Brewster without whose support and encouragement the manuscript would not have been published.

I want to thank everyone in the Department of Sociology, Bristol University, for providing me with somewhere to work in peace while preparing the manuscript and making me feel so welcome. Finally I want to thank my mother for helping out so often with child care.

Annie Phizacklea

Notes on Contributors

Floya Anthias is a lecturer in Sociology at Thames Polytechnic. Her research has largely been concerned with Cypriot social structure and Greek-Cypriot migrants in London.

Lenie Brouwer is a research worker in Amsterdam. With Marijke Priester she is currently researching the position of Turkish families in the Netherlands.

Shirley Dex is lecturer in Economics at the University of Keele. Her research has been largely concerned with generating interdisciplinary labour market theories appropriate to British black and white school-leavers.

Mary Hancock shares a job as tutor organiser for the Auckland (NZ) Workers' Educational Association. Her research has largely been concerned with the exploitation of women workers by transnational corporations and redundancy and unemployment in New Zealand.

Mirjana Morokvasic is a Research Fellow at the Centre National de la Recherche Scientifique, Paris. Her research has been largely concerned with migrant women in Western Europe. She is currently engaged on a project in collaboration with Annie Phizacklea on the clothing industry in France, Britain and West Germany.

Annie Phizacklea is a freelance researcher. Her research has been concerned with racism and migrant labour. She is currently engaged on a SSRC funded research project in collaboration with Mirjana Morokvasic.

Marijke Priester is a research worker in Amsterdam. She is currently researching the position of Turkish families in the Netherlands in collaboration with Lenie Brouwer.

Karen Stone divides her time between working in a woman's refuge in Birmingham and looking after her young children. Her research has been concerned with the relationship between motherhood, waged work and ethnicity.

Introduction

Since the Second World War, but particularly in the last fifteen years, there has been a dramatic worldwide expansion of women's participation in the waged labour force. For millions of women the transition from unwaged to waged work has come about through migration, whether it be from rural to urban areas or migration of an international kind. In this book we address both types of migration but focus in particular on the migration of women from the European periphery and Third World to the advanced industrial nations of Western Europe.

There are approximately six million women and girls in Britain, France, Belgium, the Netherlands, Switzerland, Austria, the Federal Republic of Germany and Sweden who either migrated to those countries since the 1950s or who have been born there to migrant parents. Not all will settle permanently, even if they want to, but the majority will. For the second generation there is very little choice.

The transformation of a migrant workforce into a settler population is an established fact throughout advanced industrial Western Europe (Castles, 1980a). Long before virtually all the major labour importing countries slammed their doors to the entry of new workers from outside the confines of the European Community in the early 1970s this trend was clear. Wherever possible migrant workers were avoiding return and began the process of family re-unification in the migration setting. Just as in Britain ten years earlier, this trend was stimulated by the ban on immigration.

The demand for low skill labour which had 'produced' the labour migrations from the European periphery and Third World in the 1950s and the 1960s had declined (we will look at the reasons why a little later). Having fuelled the economies of Western Europe for twenty years migrant labour now experiences staggeringly high levels of unemployment, cushioning indigenous labour against the worst effects of recession and providing a scapegoat for the problems attendant upon recession (see World Council of Churches, 1980 for a selection of press reports).

It is within this context that we begin to consider the position of migrant women workers in advanced industrial Western Europe. In the chapters which follow the reader should gain some insight into the numerous factors which act to subordinate migrant women inside and outside waged work. Many of those factors are common to all migrants and others to women

1

generally, but there still remain important differences in the
economic, politico-legal and ideological position of migrant
women when compared to either group.   As migrants they
experience racial, and in most cases legal, subordination
which act to confine them to certain types of work and rein-
force their exploitation as waged workers.   But these new
forms of oppression and exploitation are shaped and experienced in a particular way because they share with all women
subordination as a gender.   What this means in practice is
that wherever a woman comes from, wherever she migrates to,
whether or not she works, is married or has children her primary role in life will be defined not as a waged worker, but
as a mother and a domestic labourer.   It is this definition
which·is replicated and reinforced through the creation of
whole sectors of low paid, low skill 'women's work', and which
provides the basis for the much broader sexual division of
labour which is characteristic of all societies.

Women from the European periphery and the Third World
have always constituted a small but significant proportion of
the labour flow to advanced industrial Western Europe (see
Morokvasic in this volume).   But it is since the late 1960s
that their numbers have rapidly expanded.   Overall they
constitute well over a quarter of the foreign labour force, and
over 40 per cent of all migrants (Kudat and Sabancuoglu,
1980, p. 11).   Nevertheless the labour force figures are
known to be underestimates due to the high level of unregistered work amongst migrant women (ibid., p. 13; Delcourt,
1975 and Anwar, 1979).

Migrant women are disproportionately represented in the
manual sectors of women's work.   Officially this distribution
is described in the following way:

Working women in the community countries eschew employment in domestic and servile jobs in preference for service
occupations in which a greater number of openings has
become available.   There is thus room at the bottom of the
ladder· for the women immigrants to tackle the 'women's
work' (Delcourt, 1975, p. 103).

As Morokvasic points out in the next chapter this type of
comment is not restricted to official reports, but is also rife
in the extant literature on migrant women: dirty, arduous
and poorly paid work is represented as a gift from the West
to the women of the Third World.   In addition migrant women
constitute a disproportionate number of the unemployed during
periods of economic contraction (see Phizacklea in this volume).

Confined to certain sectors of the labour market because
they are women, racial discrimination and/or legal controls
intervene to ensure their subordination.   The most obvious
form of control is the work permit, issued only for jobs for
which no indigenous labour can be found (preference also
being given to European Community nationals within the
member states), or put differently, work that is shunned by

indigenous labour.   If no work permits are available or a 'waiting time' stipulated for labour market entry of spouses and dependants, there is always unregistered and highly exploitative work to be had in the informal economy (Kudat and Sabancuoglu, 1980 and Brouwer and Priester in this volume). As for racial discrimination the British experience indicates how it subordinates as effectively as the work permit system (Dex in this volume).

   These objective constraints on the nature of migrant women's work are overlaid and reinforced by the so-called 'disadvantages' that many migrant women bring with them to the labour market.   Much is made of migrant women's 'language deficiencies', 'cultural preference' and 'lack of recognised skills' in explaining migrant women's subordinate position in the labour market.   I am not suggesting that some or any of these factors do not act as objective constraints to the employment options of some migrant women.   But it must be recognised that such 'disadvantages' are used as tools for exploitation, not just by indigenous employers but by male migrant entrepreneurs as well (Wilson, 1978, Hoel, 1982 and Anthias in this volume).   While our subject matter in this volume is to analyse the position of migrant women as workers, we were all agreed that we wanted to avoid a narrow productivist approach.   Nevertheless I want to make some brief and very general comments about the context and the conditions which govern the sale of female migrant labour power in the advanced capitalist social formations of Western Europe.

   It has long been recognised that a major economic advantage of a migrant labour system is that the receiving society bears only a fraction of the reproductory costs of that labour. Firstly, in all social formations, irrespective of the migrant's politico-legal position on entry, the costs of rearing the worker are born by the country of origin.   Secondly, in those countries which operate a system of rotating migration, of young unaccompanied workers on fixed term contracts, flexibility in hiring and firing practices is guaranteed and unemployment can be exported to the country of origin. Reproductory costs are thus split up into their component parts with day-to-day maintenance taking place in the advanced capitalist countries and longer term maintenance and renewal taking place in the country of origin (Castells, 1975; Meillassoux, 1981, and Burawoy, 1980).

   In this respect it does not matter if the migrant is male or female as long as his or her length of stay can be controlled and more importantly, that family re-unification does not take place.   If this happens then the receiving society must begin to shoulder some of the reproductory costs of the worker and of his or her children.   Now this pattern of settlement is well established throughout Western Europe, thus seriously undermining a major advantage of the migrant labour system, how and why did it happen? In countries such as Britain, France and the Netherlands certain categories of colonial and ex-colonial migrant labour had the right to live and work in the metropolitan society. These workers were unaffected by the legal controls imposed on 'foreign' labour. Nevertheless, Britain and France imposed restrictions on the entry of such labour during the 1960s and 1970s and in the case of Britain this has now led to the redefinition of British citizenship. Since 1971 Britain has operated a contract labour system (Phizacklea and Miles, 1980, pp. 15-16).

It is somewhat paradoxical that while countries such as Britain were successfully eroding the right of settlement for certain categories of migrant labour, other countries, such as West Germany were grudgingly conceding the right of family re-unification. In the latter case as competition for migrant labour increased in the 1960s concessions were won through the renegotiation of bilateral agreements by the countries of emigration (Castles, 1980a).

But the economic drawbacks of settlement were not the only reasons why the entry of new workers from the European periphery and the Third World had been banned by all the major labour importing countries by 1974. The official explanation for the ban is usually the 'oil crisis', the quadrupling of oil prices in 1973 and the subsequent downturn in Western European economies. But others have suggested that the increasing militancy of migrant workers and their demands for higher pay and civil and political rights must also be considered (Cohen, 1981). And within this context the search for a cheap, flexible and 'docile' labour-force turned to the industrialising nations of the Third World; nations which can guarantee an inexhaustible supply of 'fresh' and cheap labour power through the recruitment of young, female, rural migrants 'reproduced' outside of the confines of the capitalist sector but whose productivity equals or exceeds that of their counterparts in the advanced industrial nations (see Hancock in this volume). This development has been described as the migration of capital to labour as opposed to the migration of labour to capital.

Migrant labour in Western Europe had become an unwanted and 'dangerous' element as the following quote illustrates: 'In the opinion of these governments the social and political drawbacks of immigration now seem to have become greater than the economic advantages...the fear of unrest provoked by the increasingly marginal situation of growing ethnic groups', (Organisation of Economic Co-operation and Development [OECD], 1974).

The policy adopted by Britain in the 1960s is now official policy throughout Western Europe: a ban on the further entry of workers and the introduction of measures aimed at the integration of those allowed to stay. The policy is called 'stabilisation' (Delcourt, 1975) but the reality is somewhat dif-

ferent. Harassment and arbitrary deportation remain a hall-
mark of immigration officials and police attitude and practice
to migrants, particularly those who are phenotypically distinct
(Costa-Lascoux, 1980; World Council of Churches, 1980;
Institute of Race Relations, 1979). Whatever the measures
aimed at the 'integration' of migrants (OECD, 1980) they have
been officially stamped as problematic, racism is given legislative legitimation (Miles and Phizacklea, 1979).

Alongside these developments it was possible to discern a
recomposition of the migrant labour force throughout Western
Europe. By 1977 over a million 'temporary' workers had
departed or been expelled due to recession but they had been
replaced in number by wives, husbands and children allowed
in under regulations permitting family re-unification, and by
births to foreign workers. The bulk of new 'foreign entries'
to the European labour market are now drawn from this settler population, supplemented by refugees, seasonal and fron-
tier workers (OECD, 1979 and 1980).

It is my belief that the female component of this labour
force constitutes a highly attractive form of labour power to
Western European capital, in its being both migrant and
female. Let me elaborate. Migrant and female labour share
many characteristics, both have been 'produced' by the
demand for labour in certain low-wage sectors of the economy
and they are confined to those sectors, often by specific
policies and practices which are partially justified by the
ascription of inferior characteristics, the consequence then
being viewed as vindication of the ideology (Phizacklea and
Miles, 1980, p. 14). In the case of women that inferiority
stems from the fact that their primary role is not defined as a
waged worker at all; it is defined as an actual or potential
wife and mother, economically and legally dependent upon a
male 'breadwinner'. That definition of their role has far
reaching consequences for the conditions under which they
sell their labour power. Firstly, they are paid lower wages
than men because it is assumed (whether or not they are married) that they, like migrant workers are partially dependent
upon sources other than their own wages for the costs of
their reproducton (Beechey, 1978). Secondly as Phillips and
Taylor have commented, capital 'is concerned not just with a
logic of surplus extraction but with an assertion of command it
is necessarily sensitive to those social relations which make
some workers already more subordinated than others' (1980,
p. 86). It is only within this context that we can understand how male-organised labour struggled to exclude women
from areas of waged work where they were viewed as competitors (Alexander, 1976). Also how the demand for a 'family
wage' was both consistent with this exclusionary practice and
could be justified as providing the material preconditions for
conformity to the bourgeois family form of 'male breadwinner'
and 'dependent' wife (Land, 1980).

Rather than struggle for equal pay this record of attitude
and practice amongst organised male labour has compounded
the notion of women as actual or potential domestic labourers
and as 'inferior' workers. In addition, exclusionary practice
has not meant the exclusion of women from the labour market,
but their confinement to low skill and therefore low paid
work.

We are suggesting therefore that one cannot apply pure
capital logic in explaining how this segregation arises, we
must first grasp how patriarchal ideology and practice deem
women's role as waged workers at best a secondary pre-
occupation. The strength of this ideological representation
makes few allowances for the fact that economic necessity has
always forced a proportion of married women with children to
work for wages. The scarcity of pre-school and school
holiday provision for children is consistent with the view that
the primary responsibility for child care is the mother's
(Freeman, 1982 and Stone in this volume). This factor
forces a high proportion of women to find work which enables
them to meet these responsibilities, resulting in the over-
representation of women in part-time and homeworking (West,
1982; Anthias and Brouwer and Priester in this volume).

Thus while these factors act as an overriding condition of
the sale of female labour power, indigenous and migrant
alike, there still remain important differences between the two
groups which derive from migrant status. In analysing the
effects of migrant status we are examining the relationship
between ideological and politico-legal factors. The first
layer of that relationship is between nations, between the economically dominant capitalist nations (the importers of labour)
and the economically dependent 'sending' formations. In the
case of colonial and ex-colonial social formations we are in
addition examining a situation of direct politico-ideological
domination by the metropolitan society, although economic
domination will also entail aspects of politico-ideological domination (Phizacklea and Miles, 1980, p. 10). Thus while a
major feature of the colonisation process was the development
of an ideology alleging the innate inferiority of the dominated
(Rex, 1973) it needs to be recognised that this ideology of
racism is not only directed at ex-colonial migrant labour, but
all foreign labour. Meillassoux has argued that the maintenance of racism is essential 'for the over exploitation of the so-
called under-developed peoples' and to keep the latter in a
constant state of fear (1981, p. 121; see also Castells, 1975;
Castles and Kosack, 1973, and Phizacklea in this volume).

Thus the second layer of that relationship is between
people, between migrant labour and indigenous labour and the
deep division which the ideology of racism creates between
them, resulting in exclusionary practice and the fragmentation
of the working class (Castells, 1975; Castles and Kosack,
1973; Phizacklea and Miles, 1980). Migrant women are thus

placed at the intersection of two processes, gender and racial subordination and most of the contributions in this volume attempt to analyse what this represents in a concrete form. The third layer of that relationship relates to the *de jure* politico-legal position of migrant women. In this respect migrant labour represents an extremely heterogeneous category. Nevertheless in the case of migrant women workers we can focus on two broad groupings. The first concerns women who migrate on their own for employment reasons, the vast majority of whom will be contract labour, tied to a specific job and denied civil and political rights in the migration setting. (1) These workers are by definition a highly vulnerable section of the workforce. The second category includes women and girls allowed to enter under regulations permitting family re-unification, whether or not they have a concomitant right to labour market entry varies between countries (see Phizacklea and Brouwer and Priester in this volume). If there is no such right or a 'waiting time' before legal entry is granted then they must work illegally. Illegal workers are the most vulnerable and highly exploited section of the migrant workforce (Portes, 1978). But if a woman does not resort to illegal work in these circumstances she is placed in a position of total economic dependence on her husband or father. In addition married women in this category are legally dependent on their husbands for their right of residence (Brouwer and Priester in this volume). As Wilson has remarked immigration law casts women as nothing more than 'chattels' of men (1978).

But the reasons why women migrate in the first place and why they work must be seen within this context also. Nearly all labour migration is characterised by economic compulsion due to the decomposition of backward productive sectors, principally agriculture, structural unemployment in the dependent social formations and the higher nominal and real wages offered in the dominant capitalist formation (Castells, 1975). But as Morokvasic points out in the next chapter we must recognise how this 'economic compulsion' for women may be governed by a different set of conditions to that of men. Various studies have indicated how the penetration of the cash economy in the sending societies results in women, not men, becoming a relative surplus population. Girls are thus dispatched to earn cash which they will send home in the form of remittances. In other instances female migration may be motivated by the desire to escape patriarchal oppression in the sending societies. Morokvasic's own research indicates the greater number of divorced, separated and widowed women in labour migrations in comparison with men of the same status. She points to the greater difficulties experienced by women in surviving economically with that status or changing it. Migration provides an escape route. What we are suggesting therefore is that whether we are analysing the reasons

why women migrate in search of work or whether we are analysing the reasons why migrant women take up waged work
once in the migration setting we must consider to what
degree this is an enforced situation in terms of dependency
structures within the patriarchal family.
These introductory comments aim to give the reader only a
very schematic background to the theoretical and empirical
concerns of this volume.   In the next chapter Mirjana
Morokvasic attempts a far more formidable task in assessing
the extant literature in this field.   Her presentation emphasises the poverty of conceptualisation which largely characterises the literature and that much of the work which is presented as sociological analysis is permeated by racist and
patriarchal assumptions.   In this respect I believe that this
chapter should be compulsory reading for anyone contemplat-
ing research in this field.   It raises serious questions about
the extent to which 'academic' analysis is party to, or worse,
feeds, the differing forms of oppression experienced by
migrant women in contemporary Western European social formations.   But this chapter is important in another respect -
it provides the first systematic critique of the literature at an
international level, thus making a major contribution to the
sharing of information.   As the author points out this exchange of accumulated knowledge is very limited, particularly
beyond national frontiers and severely restricts the potential
theoretical advances that can be made in this field.
This chapter is followed by three contributions which focus
on different aspects of the British situation.   First, Karen
Stone presents an in-depth study of the employment situation
of mothers drawn from three ethnic groups, West Indian,
Asian and white women (mainly British) all of whom have at
least one child aged six years or younger.   The study examines the employment position of the three groups of women
and considers the effects of sexual and racial oppression.
Her in-depth interview material with the women is supplemented by a survey of child-care facilities locally and a survey of
local employment opportunities.   While Stone shows how
racial discrimination and, in the case of Asian mothers, cultural constraints, act as additional obstacles to the employment
options of black women, all of the working women in the
sample share the same confinement to low paid, low status
and gender-specific work.   In addition they all share a similar consciousness of children, rather than pure gender or
racial discrimination, as the major constraint on their employment options.   But despite this overriding similarity there
are consistent differences between the three groups of women
in their perceptions of the dual role of wage worker and
mother.   The differing rates of economic activity between the
three groups cannot be explained with reference to the differences in the economic circumstances of the families.   The
marked contrast in the women's perception of the wage and

family finance organisation is shown to lie in differences in
the perception of gender roles and definitions of motherhood
between the three ethnic groups.
  Shirley Dex's chapter on the labour market experiences of
second generation West Indian girls leads to some very similar
conclusions.   Unemployment amongst black youth in Britain
has reached staggeringly high levels in the last few years,
yet because the notion of the 'male breadwinner' remains
ideologically supreme, little or no attention is paid to the fate
of the young black women who constitute half of that 'youth'
population.   The large-scale longitudinal survey data upon
which this analysis is based was commissioned by the Department of Employment and we would hope that the results will
be given the attention they deserve in official circles.   In
the face of almost complete lack of official concern, this chapter bears testimony to the resilience and determination of
young black women to overcome the gender and racial discrimination which confronts them in British labour markets.
Dex's analysis shows that if we take educationally matched
young black and white women, we find the black women last
in the hiring queue and first in the firing queue.   The West
Indian mother supplies a strong and positive role model for
her daughter who is far more employment orientated than her
white counterpart, but racial discrimination intervenes.   In
these circumstances it might be expected that young black
women would react by simply withdrawing from the labour
market.   But they do not withdraw, a strategy in keeping
with their mothers' tradition of self-reliance.   This self-
reliance is not an inherited, biological characteristic (West
Indian women are not 'naturally' like this), but a response to
a certain set of structural features and related experience.
In short, young West Indian women are waging their own
struggle in the face of very severe difficulties in Britain
today.
  The next chapter draws our attention to an increasingly
common development throughout Western Europe, the achievement of a petit-bourgeois class position by migrant men at the
expense of migrant women.   Focusing on Greek-Cypriots in
London, Floya Anthias examines the way in which Greek-
Cypriot women's labour has been used as the cornerstone of
the Greek-Cypriot ethnic economy in Britain.   In analysing
the position of rural women in Cyprus at the time of emigration and then drawing on her own research in London she
shows how Cypriot female migrant labour provided a pool of
often unpaid or at least cheap labour for the small-scale
entrepreneurial activities of Cypriot men.   She argues that
this has involved the direct extension of production for use
into production for exchange and the extension of the patriarchal relations of the family into wage labour.   Despite
women gaining some degree of financial independence she
argues that their subordination to Cypriot male authority

remains great.   Nevertheless she concludes on a more optimistic note in respect of the second generation of Cypriot
women whom she sees as learning to manage the cultural,
moral and sexual contradictions which confront them in
Britain.

In my own contribution to this book I widen the focus of
analysis to examine the class position of migrant women
generally in the British, French and West German social formations.   The position of migrant women in economic,
politico-legal and ideological relations is compared to that of
indigenous women.   While their position in these three sets
of relations is in many respects similar to working women
generally, it is sufficiently distinct to warrant the description
of a 'fractionalised' class position.

In the final part of the chapter I suggest that the self-
organisation and struggle of migrant women both inside and
outside the work place should be analysed with reference to
this class position.   In addition I argue that it is crucial in
the present economic and political conjuncture that the issues
raised by migrant women themselves are materially and morally
supported as class issues.

Lenie Brouwer and Marijke Priester raise a different set of
questions in their study of Turkish women in their homeland
and in the migration setting.   Taking the sexual division of
labour as a power relationship in which women are controlled
by men, mediated by ideology, their detailed ethnographic
analysis explores this control in the spheres of gender identity, marriage and labour (both domestic and waged).   The
great strength of their analysis is that it is based on fieldwork in both Turkey and Amsterdam which allows them to
analyse migration in terms of different control mechanisms of
men over women.

Their conclusions once more put into question a prevalent
assumption in the extant literature which suggests that participation in the production process as wage labourers must
lead to 'emancipation' for migrant women.   Rather their findings support those of Karen Stone, in that any evaluation of
the effects of wage labour, must take into account the intricate system of power relations and control mechanisms within
the family.   Migration and wage earning does not weaken
male control over these Turkish women, to the contrary it
intensifies it.

Finally we turn to that development often described as
'capital to labour, rather than labour to capital' or the reloca-
tion of labour intensive manufacturing industries to the low-
wage industrialising zones of the world.   We have suggested
that this development has acted as a major economic factor in
the turnabout of labour migration to advanced industrial
Western Europe.   What is rarely recognised is that this
development represents a new labour migration, a migration of
young women raised outside the confines of the capitalist

sector.   Mary Hancock's analysis is based on a cross-cultural study of transnational corporations in the First World and their impact on Third World countries.   She shows how the targetting of women as a cheap labour force has been a key factor in the development of transnational production with its movement to offshore production sites in less developed, Third World countries.   Her research, based on the electronics industry, leads to an unwelcome conclusion.   As the electronics industry is one of the key areas of growth in the world economy, current trends would tend to indicate that this exploitation of women, particularly as assembly workers in offshore sites, will increase as more corporations, particularly from advanced industrial Western Europe, move in search of cheap labour.

The volume does not represent a single theoretical 'line'. Early in our group discussions we agreed to adopt the conceptualisation of migrant women workers as the bearers of a triple burden - as women, as migrants and as workers.   But beyond this we recognised that the imposition of a single theoretical approach necessitated eight individuals adopting an agreed position within what constitutes ongoing debates in two fairly discrete areas of interest - one on women and waged work, the other on labour migration.   These ongoing debates do not merely represent academic differences of opinion; they represent real political differences in debate and practice.

Thus we make no apology for leaving certain theoretical issues unresolved.   If we succeed in stimulating debate in this area, raise questions about the adequacy of extant theory and most importantly increase awareness of the oppression and exploitation experienced by migrant women workers then we will have achieved our principal aims.

NOTES

1 There are obvious exceptions, for example the Irish in Britain have the same *de jure* politico-legal rights as British citizens.   New Commonwealth women entering prior to 1962 or after that date as dependants (until 1973) also continue to have the same politico-legal rights as the indigenous population except with respect to the rights of certain dependants to live with them.   Nevertheless it is vital to recognise that Britain has operated a contract labour system since 1971.

1 Women in migration: beyond the reductionist outlook

Mirjana Morokvasic

Women play an important economic and demographic role in contemporary migrations not only in Europe but throughout the world. This seems to be only a recently acknowledged fact, although the evidence for it existed well over a decade ago: a UN document based on comparative European labour market and population statistics collected around 1970 clearly indicates that 'the overall activity rates of migrants were higher than among the indigenous population and that this was particularly true among women' ('Labour Supply and Migration in Europe', 1979, p. 125). But it is precisely in the period for which this first comparative statistical evidence exists that there are hardly any studies on migrant women. At that time they were still sociologically invisible, although numerically and socially present. Then, gradually (in particular in the second half of the seventies), issues related to the position of migrant women began to be considered and a 'literature' as such emerged.

This chapter is an attempt to distinguish and classify various trends in the literature concerning women and migration. There is, of course, a literature in which migrant women are totally absent: in the general theories of migration, migrants are usually sex-less units; if they are constructed into sociological objects then they are male and a considerable number of studies have used exclusively male samples. This deliberate exclusion of women is usually justified by the lack of research funds and by women's supposedly minor economic role. The second trend I consider in this chapter (which is more or less contemporary with that which excluded women) marked the first step in taking migrant women out of their sociological invisibility. A number of investigations mentioned women within the framework of the family, and in relation to children. This literature relies on stereotypes of migrant women as dependants, migrants' wives or mothers, unproductive, illiterate, isolated, secluded from the outside world and the bearers of many children. It is a literature shaped by selecting a certain number of characteristics observed in a limited number of migrant women. These characteristics are usually attributed to the women's alleged 'cultural backgrounds' and commonly labelled as 'tradition'. Needless to say the stereotype operates for *all* migrant women irrespective of their specific national and cultural origins.

But migrant women acquired the right to a sociological

existence once they were acknowledged as economically active, as productive.   Admitted as active protagonists within the migratory movements, they were analysed as persons in their own right for the first time in a literature that started to appear from around the mid-seventies onwards.   In the context of migratory labour movements the predominant stereotype of migrant women as economically inactive had reduced the issue of women to the level of triviality and of no importance.   It is therefore understandable that they could acquire a status of 'social actor' only by opposition to the existing stereotype.   However, one may legitimately ask why only the economically active women migrants should be 'sociologisable' (considered worthy of sociological analysis)?   This literature on migrant women has redressed the existing imbalance and has had an undeniable merit in highlighting one so far neglected aspect of the migratory phenomenon. Nevertheless, the majority of the authors in this trend do not break with the tradition of stereotyping and common sense. They adopt a 'psycho-culturalist' approach in which the objects of investigation are migrant women as individuals, their migration determined by individual motivation and desires and their condition analysed within a perspective of adaptation to the 'host society' formulated in terms of an evolution towards some 'emancipated' state.

There are in contrast a number of studies, although also partially focusing on individual women, which detach themselves from this outlook and often put it openly in question. The final section of this chapter is devoted to the process of female migration and the way in which various studies have analysed the determinants of female migration and the sex selectivity in the migratory movements.

ABSENT

Migratory movements under certain circumstances and in certain contexts concern men only or predominantly, in others women tend to predominate.   Migration is a sex selective process.   But for a long time in the literature it appeared as a male affair only, a process from which women were excluded. Researchers found it justified to investigate all-male samples or to propose general theories and models based on surveys of male migrants.   This happened not only in contexts where the sex ratio in the migratory movements was in favour of males - as in most countries in Europe particularly in the sixties - but also in other contexts where women outnumbered men.   In Mexico for instance and in Latin America generally women predominate in rural to urban migration:

Migration in Latin America can hardly be described as an under-studied phenomenon, yet within the vast body of literature in various disciplines about migration few have paid

particular attention to female migration although as most of
the studies show female migration to the cities is considerably greater than that of males (Young, 1980, p. 1).
Browning and Feindt's study of migration to Monterey,
Mexico, completely excludes women (1971) while other studies
of Latin American migration acknowledge women's presence
and yet also virtually ignore it in their analyses (Sandis,
1971; Price, 1971; and Moore, 1971). As Cohen (1977)
points out this leads to a situation where women play a central role in the movements of peoples in the Americas yet they
are neglected in the sphere of policy and their impact on the
American economy has not been adequately assessed. Cohen
confirms statements of the kind made earlier in the European
context and repeated often thereafter: 'In the literature on
migration the presence of migrant women is seldom related to
production so that their economic function remains neglected'
(Morokvasic, 1974, p. 6). A similar exclusion of women from
both the literature and migration policy considerations takes
place in other parts of the world too. Palmer (1979), com-
menting on Africa, suggests that 'in spite of the pronounced
female migration most of the commentary on motives for migration refer to men' (p. 46).
    In Europe, Lawrence's study on race relations in Britain
(1974) was based on a representative sample of male Commonwealth coloured immigrants in Nottingham. The author does
not say why he drew males only from the electoral lists.
Shirley Dex's chapter in this volume draws attention to other
British studies which either exclude or virtually ignore the
presence of migrant women. The authors of 'The Seventh
Man' (Berger and Mohr, 1975) limit themselves to migrant men
in Western Europe, but they are exceptional insofar as they
recognise this as a limitation and express their hope that a
corresponding piece of research about women in migration
would be published soon.

MIGRANTS' WIVES: THE STEREOTYPE

It is sometimes difficult to draw a clear line between the literature which excludes women completely and that in which they
are mentioned only as an accessory of a process they are not
really taking part in. 'Migrants' is a broad category cover-
ing a wide range of subtypes and subcategories. While the
migrant could be either male or female, it has been shown
above that it is more common to refer to a migrant as male.
In particular in the usual expression 'migrants and their families', 'families' are understood to be composed of dependent
members, women and children, while the 'migrant' is considered to be a male breadwinner. Whether this is a genuine or
only an ascribed dependency the division into migrants (male)
and dependants has served as a basic guideline in recording

statistics and in policy-making. In research it has contributed to creating and perpetuating the invisibility of migrant
women. In important works on migration, the symbolic references to women as migrants' wives and their stereotypical
presentation as wives and mothers has led to a conceptualisation of migrant women as followers, dependants, unproductive
persons, isolated, illiterate and ignorant. In this kind of
literature, sociologically, migrant women are only visible
within the framework of the family.

Minces (1973) at one point in his book on foreign workers
in France completely ignores women: 'Men alone were brought
to this country in which the family is glorified' (p. 433, my
translation). Further on in the text he presents a stereotype generalised to all migrant women;

She [the migrant woman] does not speak the language of
the host country; of course she generally does not read or
write and, since she does not work, she has not her own
resources; above all she has no real possibility of getting
into contact with the industrial world in which she lives.
Finally, feeling hostility, she will frequently live in an even
more restrained milieu than in her country, meeting usually
only women, her neighbours, of the same age and the same
socio-cultural level (ibid., p. 433, my translation).

Granotier (1971, 1979) relegates migrant women to half a
page, in both the first and the revised version of his sociological study of migrant workers in France. For him migrant
women are excluded from the production process and, except
for some, 'the job, a privileged mode of adaptation does not
exist for them' (1971, p. 85). The author confuses the mode
of their arrival, via the family immigration channel, with the
reality of their stay in France. Their entry as a 'spouse'
immediately excludes for that author, the possibility of their
access to the labour market. 'Work is the privileged mode of
adaptation to the society around them. The majority of
women, however, arrive only through the family immigration
channel and for them the risks of isolation are greater' (1971,
p. 145; 1979, p. 165). This is a somewhat strange
approach to be adopted in a sociological study, particularly
as official evidence existed concerning the economic activity
rates of married migrant women. The small amount of attention devoted to migrant women by this author is to define
them in terms of social problems and not in terms of sociological questions: 'The necessity of learning the language is
felt less than by their husbands ... she has difficulties of
insertion into the French context' (1971, p. 85); 'Certain
social services attempt to teach them the rudiments of French
and even some home economics. But only a small number of
them can be reached' (ibid., p. 145).

The stereotype of migrant women is formulated in the most
elaborate way in Valabregue (1973). The whole book is
devoted to migrants in France in general and a few chapters

concern women more specifically. The condition of migrant
women (again in general terms) is analysed from the perspective of adaptation to French society. The approach is
explicitly ethnocentric: women are evaluated in terms of
their capacity of access to modernity, i.e. to be 'promoted'
and thereby be better adapted. Their social reality is re-
constructed on the basis of the common-sense stereotype
which situates migrant women at one end of the tradition-
modernity dichotomy. The stereotype selects the traits from
a hypothetical, or rather, reconstructed cultural inventory:
the woman is isolated, subjugated to the husband's will, any
attempt to overcome isolation is met with the husband's dis-
approval or veto. The migrant family and woman's role
within it becomes problematic from the point of view of adaptation to modern French society. On a scale of capacity of
access to modernity the most conservative and the most imper-
meable to the 'enlightening modern influences' are the Algerian
families and Algerian women. The two fundamental criteria
of access to modernity are employment and contraception – the
doors to progress and liberation: contraception (birth control
is in this type of literature reduced to contraceptives only)
becomes a pedagogical tool which stimulates progress in other
domains (ibid., p. 125). Accepting pregnancy regulation
plays a primary role in promoting these underdeveloped women
(ibid., p. 124). The author not only describes migrant
women as 'underdeveloped' but assumes that pregnancy regulation is something no migrant woman has thought of before
coming to France. Interestingly for Valabregue, the first
stage in the learning of modernity is taking place in the
modern kitchen (p. 131) where the young Algerian girls are
learning their way out of *their* oppressive traditions by preparing the food *à la française*.
  But the view that home economics is an essential element in
'adaptation' is not confined to sociologists such as Granotier
and Valabregue, it is the core of many training programmes
for migrant women: 'Their purpose is to promote women so
that they can play fully the role for which they are made, the
one of helpmate, of housewife and of educator' (Hommes et
Migrations, 1971, p. 14). Such programmes, devised with
the best of intentions to help some unspecified immigrant
woman 'adapt' to the new society, do in fact patronise her.
Her background is ignored and she is treated as a complete
tabula rasa in terms of cooking, taking care of children,
finding sensible food, sewing ... Western ways are better
ways ....
  The approach adopted by Zahraoui in his study of Algerian
families (1976) is different insofar as it presents the situation
'from within' and not from a perspective of an outsider.
However, as far as women are concerned, they are no more
visible than in other studies of this kind. The presence of
women makes it possible for a researcher to speak about the

family instead of speaking about Algerian workers only.   But
the woman remains silent and invisible, present as a variable,
absent as a person.   The family has one voice and one
spokesman: the man.   It could be argued that the author as
a man and as an investigator had this one-sided access to the
family, but as a sociologist he should at least recognise the
necessity of decoding this type of interaction between himself
and the family members instead of presenting a family as an
entity, where the head of the family becomes synonymous with
the family.   The absence of women in this analysis of the
family drives the author to the usual stereotyped conclusion:
the woman, isolated both in her own family and in the 'host'
society (ibid., p. 150).

The absence of migrant women or their inadequate stereotypical representation as dependants has been justified by
their 'genuine invisibility' which was then in turn attributed
to the women's cultural origins.   In the absence of any
knowledge of the specific cultural backgrounds of the women
in question, the image of migrant women was shaped by
making generalisations about all migrant women from the group
perceived as culturally the most removed.   'Culture' then
becomes a rag-bag in which one puts what one wants and
takes out what best suits the author's argumentation.

Further attention to the biased representation of migrant
women in sociological literature is not necessary.   It was
mentioned here because this approach was typical of a certain
period of time;   it still exists but is no longer predominant.
The authors who adopted this approach failed to distance
themselves from unverified assumptions based on stereotypes
and perhaps more seriously reinforced them.   While justifying
the absence of migrant women from their research or categor-
ising them as unproductive, the same authors projected on to
migrant women their own, only partially rejected image of
women generally as invisible and socially (thereby sociologically) not important or not worth investigating.   It is important to present this approach because it perpetuates itself
later, even in the literature which has explicitly questioned
the stereotype, but does not eliminate it.   On the contrary
it has incorporated it as an element of its own 'different'
approach.   Many of the subsequent studies on migrant
women, while giving them the status of 'social actor', have
maintained the tradition-modernity polarization in which the
'modern' values (whatever the precautions the author takes)
are supposed to be the emancipatory ones.

A RECOGNISED PRESENCE: IMMIGRANT WOMEN

Most researchers who have focused their attention on migrant
women from the mid-seventies onwards acknowledge their previous invisibility in research, and the inadequacy of previous

approaches (Morokvasic, 1974, 1975; Levi, 1977; Leonetti
and Levi, 1979; Allen, 1980; Hoffman-Nowotny, 1977; to
mention just a few). These are the researchers whose own
early work in the field of migration had suffered to some
extent from the 'sexist myopia which ran through almost all
the published work on migrants' (Allen, 1979, p. 4). The
image of migrant women as dependants and followers of men
contributed to perpetuating their invisibility until the mid-
seventies. The emergence of a literature on migrant women
owes much to two circumstances: one is a wider feminist
questioning about women's role in society, the other is a
recognition of migrant women as economically important.
    The first influence is self-evident and though not all the
works which have appeared since 1975 could be labelled as
feminist the fact that sociology has turned to women in
general as actors (protagonists) in the social reality has also
had its impact on the sociology of migration. The charge
made that migrant women are seldom discussed as people in
their own right (Morokvasic, 1974; Billiet, 1974; Churches
Committee on Migrant Workers, 1974, etc.) was followed up by
action at the level of international organisations, and agencies, each devoting one or more of their sessions to the
issues concerning migrant women from around 1975 onwards.
Several specialised and other journals had issues on the subject of migrant women ('New Community', 'Anthropological
Quarterly', and 'Migrants Formation'). Films were made:
'Femmes immigrees', 'Shirin's Hochzeit', 'Il valore della Donna
e il suo silenzio' ('Immigrant Women', 'Shirin's Wedding', 'The
Highest Value of a Woman is her Silence').
    Attempts to redress the imbalance in the literature were of
various kinds. Most felt that the first thing to do was to
point to the official statistics and reveal migrant women as
important economically (Morokvasic, 1974; Billiet, 1974;
Majava, 1974). Other studies, which could be labelled as
pioneering descriptive works, drew attention to the unreliabil-
ity of official data and to the under-estimation of migrant
women's role. The abundant literature that started appear-
ing from the mid-seventies onwards (see bibliography by
Münscher, 1980; Taravella, 1980) has had an undeniable
merit in highlighting one so far neglected dimension of migration. This new approach was certainly useful in making
migrant women more adequately known and has contributed to
a better understanding of the migratory process as a whole.
Nevertheless, there are serious theoretical shortcomings with
much of this work.

Immigrant women: a psycho-culturalist perspective

The majority of works that appeared in the second half of the
seventies can be classified under this subheading. There is

a radical shift of focus from the family and migrant women as
dependants to other spheres, in particular, their role as
waged workers.   On the one hand, this approach has suc-
ceeded in correcting the previous one based on stereotypes,
but on the other it has used the stereotype as an explanatory variable in its own analysis.   The main characteristics
and shortcomings of this approach are an emphasis on individual characteristics, the lack of a broader theoretical perspective, the lack of a comparative approach and the absence
of reference to the background of migrant women.

While female migrants become assessed as workers in this
approach, female migration fails to be related to the migratory movements of labour and their determinants.   As a consequence, migrant women are assessed as individuals whose
behaviour is above all determined by their psychology and
their 'culture'.   They are approached from the perspective
of adaptation to the 'host' society, whether the author is
cautious and speaks of 'insertion' instead of adaptation or,
more frequently, focuses on change and on the 'emancipatory'
effects of the migration of women.   Access to paid work and
to contraception are seen by most authors as the prerequis-
ites for that change.

But when speaking about change one needs a point of reference.   Since most of the studies do not make any adequate
reference to the background of the women they claim to examine, this background is reconstructed on the basis of the
existing stereotype.   In other words, the stereotype of a
traditional oppressed, isolated woman who does not work and
is constantly pregnant, is not abandoned; it is on the contrary adopted and fixed in some more or less recent past of
migrant women.   'Change' is then evaluated in relation to
that past: there are women who change and those who resist
it.   They change thanks to modern influences which reach
them either through the mass media or through contacts with
the bourgeoisie;   if they resist it is because of strong 'traditional barriers' to modern life.   It is interesting to note that
researchers in various parts of the world attribute to migrant
women of extremely different origins one and the same simpli-
fied cultural background and label it 'tradition', meaning
immobility and oppression of women, and oppose it to their
own average western model of modernity.   Again, as in the
studies based on stereotypes, migrant women are placed on
the tradition to modernity continuum: the women's path on
the continuum is sometimes a zigzagging, sometimes a straight
one, but they are all unmistakably striving for the Western,
modern and, of course, emancipatory values.   If they don't,
they become problem persons for their entourage and problem
cases for native social workers to deal with.

Having in mind such a hypothetical migrant woman coming
from a condition of unshaken roots and unchallenged values,
i.e. point zero of change, most authors have tried to answer

the inevitable question: What does migration do to them?
The assumptions about 'change' are based on the findings of
studies on urbanisation and the effects of access of women to
employment. Hess-Buechler (1976) clearly specifies the conditions under which some change might take place and this
passage summarises some of the common assumptions about the
emancipatory impact of the migratory process on women:

Migration per se does not account for major differences in
the position of women unless it is accompanied by changes
in her reproductive role through family planning and her
productive role in terms of control of strategic resources
and education (Introduction, Special Issue, 'Anthropological
Quarterly', vol. 49).

The underlying assumption is - although not explicit - that
there was no family planning before emigration and that the
productive role of women would be changed in the direction of
increased control over economic resources. 'Change' in this
type of research is conceptualised as a passage (an evolution)
from tradition to modernity, modernity being always synonymous with promotion, betterment and freedom for women.
Work is envisaged as an element of modernity, non-existent
as a norm or as a behaviour before emigration took place.

Lebon, for instance, implies that migrant women may be
adopting the model of French women for whom the norm is to
work outside the home (1979). The tradition-modernity
dichotomy is explicit in the title of a paper by Cirba and
Costa-Lascoux, 'du role traditionnel au travail salarie' ('from
a traditional role to waged work', 1980). While the authors
refute the dichotomy in a sentence in their paper they nevertheless use it in their argument about the 'recent' increase in
economic activity among migrant women. Migrant women's
access to waged work is seen only in terms of an abandonment
of an attributed norm of non-work. Waged work is represented as a gift of Western societies to the women of the Third
World and as a remedy to their struggle against their oppressive traditions.

As a consequence the attribution of the status of the waged
worker to migrant women does not lead to a class analysis.
This status is only seen in functionalist terms as a .step
towards emancipation. According to Hoffman-Nowotny,
'already in the first generation of immigrant women a distinct
impetus towards emancipation makes itself felt' (1977, p.22).
The author bases his analysis on data for Switzerland and on
a Eurocentric theory of roles and statuses. Referring to
Held and Levy's statement for Switzerland as a whole, which
argues that 'where a woman is working traditionality is lower
than where a woman is not working' (1976, p. 162) the author
concludes that 'regardless of the fact that the immigrant
woman is at a disadvantage concerning stratum, her occupational activity will still affect the sphere of primary discrimination.... Woman's position in the family will be strengthened.'

Likewise, Foner states that 'regardless of other drawbacks that residence in England has for Jamaican women, the chance to earn a regular wage has led to a dramatic improvement in their lives' (1979, p. 83).   Other authors affirm too that 'with acquisition of some economic independence these women have a stronger position to demand emancipation from their traditional subordinate role' (Castles and Kosack, 1973, p. 362).   Kosack (1976) assumes that being actively involved in the production process, having the same power as all produc- tive workers and getting involved in struggles are the pre- conditions for migrant women's emancipation and Ley (1979) sees in migration to Switzerland a trend towards more egali- tarian relationships within the family.

Levi (1977) indicates the direction of change that she assumes would take place thanks to the work contacts of Portuguese women: 'The jobs that they have are mostly those of domestic servants which put them into contact with the bourgeoisie whose values and behaviour they have the possi- bility of perceiving,' (p. 287).   Similarly, Abadan-Unat (1977), who writes on the situation of Turkish women in Ger- many, views emancipation as closely related to the process of modernisation (p. 36).   The author develops a set of criteria for measuring emancipation: decline of extended family rela- tions and adoption of nuclear family patterns, fragmentation of family structure, entrance into wage earning, mass media exposure, decline of religious practices, increasing belief in egalitarian opportunities of girls and boys, adoption of con- sumption behaviour.   Abadan-Unat, like Katarina Ley (1979), warns about drawbacks, what she calls 'pseudoemancipation' and says that the entrance of migrant women into urban jobs may not always produce the 'expected gradual emancipation' (ibid., p. 54).   Abadan-Unat sees the causes for this failure to emancipate in women themselves and in their reticent atti- tudes to modernity: as long as they do not accept entry into employment for good, but only as a temporary expedient, un- desired and not sought after, 'many of the natural (sic) con- sequences of urban occupation might fall short' (p. 54). Clearly, for the author an urban woman with a job is an emancipated one;   from that is derived that 'German women have a higher degree of emancipation than the Turkish' (ibid., p. 41).

Not all the authors present the polarized tradition-modernity continuum in such explicit terms.   But within the evolutionist perspective it is difficult to avoid the evaluation of change and in doing so, inevitably, grade the emancipation and oppression of women 'here', as opposed to 'there', from the understanding that there is less oppression here in the West and more there in some reified 'traditional background'. Leonetti and Levi (1979) in their analysis of immigrant women in France do not avoid the tradition-modernity perspective. Although the explicit objective of the authors is not the study of change, but the study of migrant women's 'insertion' into French society, change becomes, nevertheless, indispensable to an understanding of the process of 'insertion' (integration). They need a point of reference for evaluating change, so, at the beginning of their study they provide a schematic description of the condition and status of women in 'traditional societies', those of Maghreb and those of the Iberian peninsula.   This approach produces a static image of societies which are in the process of rapid change.   It eradicates the differences between the countries and within the countries, as well as regional, ethnic and class differences.   While the authors attempt to carefully construct the immigrant woman's background they end up with the 'traditional societies as a point of reference, unshaken roots and unquestioned values' to which they oppose modern French society as less oppressive and more advanced.   Since the starting point for the authors is cultural immobility and lack of change, then, for them, putting the women's roles into question shakes the whole cultural system itself (p. 253).

Whether the authors arrive at the conclusion that migration emancipates, pseudo-emancipates or strengthens the 'traditional ties', whether the evolution from tradition to modernity is considered a unilinear path or not, whether it is explicit or surrounded with a number of cautious remarks, the point of departure and the point of arrival remain the same for all these authors.   Work as an 'attribute of modern society' is therefore a mediator, a facilitator in the transition to modernity.

Two common traits can be distinguished as characteristics of the works quoted so far in this section: first, 'tradition' becomes a substitute for an analysis of migrant women's specific socio-cultural background and second, they lack any definition of migrant women as a category of analysis.

The a-historical approach in migration studies in general has already been criticised by Sayad in his analysis of Algerian emigration: 'Any study neglecting the conditions of origin of the emigrants would be condemned to produce a partial and ethnocentric view of migratory phenomenon' (1977, p. 59). Indeed, women migrants are treated only as immigrants, their lives analysed from the moment they enter the new country. The stereotype of 'traditional women' implies that migrant women are tabulae rasae as regards certain norms and behaviour (such as birth control and access to waged work) attributed to the immigrant society, and any difference from the stereotype is interpreted as a change towards the adoption of new models (supposed to be promoting, liberating, emancipatory).

At the same time, migrant women as a category of analysis remains loosely defined.   Although several authors insist on the articulation between class, gender and immigrant status (Morokvasic, 1974;   Kosack, 1976;   Hoffman-Nowotny, 1977;

Allen, 1979;   Leonetti and Levi, 1979) this combination is
rarely taken into account when considering the effects of
migration.   The focus remains rather on gender only and
the changes concern primarily, if not exclusively, gender
relationships in isolation from other relationships within the
social structure.   Therefore the attribution of the status of
a worker to migrant women has not led to the analysis of the
labour process or to a class analysis, it is simply seen as a
variable in promoting change.
  The tendency to focus on individual migrant women is described by Leeds as 'a reductionist and individualistic outlook...
the migration phenomenon is not properly intelligible in terms
of individuals at all' (1976, pp. 69 and 71).
  Some authors reject Leeds's view as unjustified (Thadani
and Todaro, 1978;   Rogers, 1976).   Indeed, to deny the
utility of carrying out research on women migrants means
ignoring the specific function of gender: used universally as
a criterion of social stratification and discrimination.   This
is highly relevant to migratory movements where women are
being introduced as an important facet, if not the main component (see Mary Hancock's chapter in this book) of a mobile
and cheap labour force, enabling capital to maximise profits.
  Leeds is, nevertheless, right in arguing that the migratory
processes, and in particular their determinants, cannot be explained in terms of individual motives and drives.   We shall
see in the following section on female migration how some
authors have gone beyond this individualistic explanation of
female migrations.   It is also true that the situation of
migrant women cannot be analysed only in terms of their
gender and, as Leeds says, 'being a woman is simply only one
of a set of discriminatory criteria' (1976, p. 74).   As mentioned above, a number of authors have drawn attention to
the articulation of the discriminatory criteria concerning
women, but only a few have taken this articulation into
account when analysing the processes of change and inter-
preting them.
  A number of studies, although also focusing on migrants as
individuals, have overcome either one or both characteristics
of the reductionist outlook.   The approach adopted varies
considerably from one study to another.

BEYOND...

Pioneering descriptive case studies

A considerable amount of work in this field is based on case
studies and on biographic material, a necessary approach in a
new area.   It provides invaluable first-hand information not
only on the family, the most usual sphere of sociological visibility for migrant women, but also on other features of their

stay abroad.   In most of these studies the author provides a
detailed analysis of the background of one or several cases
analysed.   The life-history approach, present in most of
these works, provides for the interpretation of migrant
women's current conditions abroad.   Kamenko's (1978) and
Arondo's (1975) cases are presented in the form of an autobiog-
raphy.   Baumgartner-Karabak and Landesberger (1978) and
Lacoste-Dujardin (1976) incorporate in their analyses both the
background conditions (Anatolia and Kabillie) and the present
conditions abroad (Berlin and Paris).   Van Mannen (1979)
uses a similar procedure to the one adopted in Berger and
Mohr (1975):   her photographs show the condition of migrant
women in various parts of Holland.   No words could describe
so well the nineteenth-century conditions experienced by
migrant women in advanced, capitalist Holland.   Wilson's
'Finding a Voice' (1978), based on the case studies of women
from the Indian subcontinent, examines the oppressive conditions experienced by women both at home and at work, their
isolation in a hostile and racist society and finally their own
ways of fighting back (a necessary corrective to the image of
the 'passive' migrant woman).   These works are mentioned
separately because they do not have any deeper analytical
ambitions and do not aim at further theoretical generalisations.
Their aim is to inform and to describe, to put together various experiences.   They have admirably fulfilled this task.

Class analysis

Phizacklea (1982) points out that there 'has been little attempt
to analyse the class position of migrant women workers, nor
the forms of consciousness and action that they have brought
into the arena of working class struggle' (p. 99).   Her analysis focuses on West Indian women in Britain and their position in economic, politico-legal and ideological relations.   She
concludes that they constitute a racially and sexually categorised fraction of the working class and demonstrate corresponding forms of consciousness and action.

Studying networks

Saifullah-Khan (1974, 1976, 1979) is one of the few researchers
who devotes as much attention to the background of migrants
as to their present position.   This is the only way of avoiding ethnocentricity in the analysis and in the interpretations
which tend to phrase the position of foreign women essentially
in terms of Western values, with emphasis on individuality.
Saifullah-Khan's work was carried out in two different parts of
England characterised by different structural constraints
imposed on Asian women of similar origins.   Her work

emphasises the very elastic boundaries of ethnicity which then differently define what is appropriate behaviour and what is not (including the access of women to economic activity under differing conditions).   For Khan the social networks of Asian women act as a system of support and information sharing particularly in relation to job-seeking.   For Andezian and Streiff (1981), whose work also focuses on networks of migrant women but reaches opposite conclusions, boundaries of acceptance for North African women in Marseilles remain restricted and the authors do not even try to envisage the functioning of women's networks other than as a mechanism of social control over the preservation of a certain number of norms and behaviours.   In that respect, their analysis, although innovative and interesting, remains often an apology for the status quo.

A fourfold oppression

Most studies have focused on migrant women as individuals and in analysing their position the emphasis has been on gender.   I have argued elsewhere (Morokvasic, 1980) that there is a need to establish the link between the individual migrant and the migratory process on one hand, and to re-define migrant women as a category of analysis, on the other. The approach adopted in my own study of Yugoslav migrant women in France, Germany and Sweden (Morokvasic, 1980 and forthcoming) attempts to meet this double objective: the displacement of women is related to migratory movements of labour in an attempt to highlight the social forces or constraints that have so far remained hidden behind the common explanations of female migration in terms of individual drives. Special attention has been paid to the background of the migrant women studied and this, together with the comparative approach adopted in that investigation, provides for a more accurate interpretation of the effects of the migratory process on migrant women workers.

   To be able to understand what happens to migrant women - and considering that studying changes should not be a taboo matter - one has to look beyond gender.   In some studies on migrant women their condition has been defined as a triple burden or triple oppression at the level of class, gender and migrant minority group member.   The empirical evidence and the discussion on effects were, however, focused on gender. In my own work the condition of migrant women was defined as a fourfold oppression.   It was assumed that women were not only subjected and discriminated against because they were women, working class and members of a migrant minority group, but also because they may accept this as their fate, as natural and as normal.   It was also assumed that migrant women stand a better chance of reacting to any of the three forms of oppression if they do not carry the oppression within themselves. It was not assumed however that possible reactions would necessarily take a form familiar to a Western observer or be directed against the issues predictable from a Western frame of reference.

The study attempted to answer the question 'can migratory experiences provide conditions under which women could gain awareness that their position is not fated and/or can it provide conditions under which these women could fight their oppression and how?' Yugoslavs, due to their origins, were likely to be aware that their condition is not fated and that it can be changed, in other words they are less likely to accept the status quo as inevitable and as worth preserving. The historically and culturally heterogeneous origin of the Yugoslavs with an institutional background very different from the vast majority of other emigration areas (institutionalised equality, progressive laws, access of women to the public sphere and to employment) places them in theory in an exceptional position as compared with other migrant women. In other words, Yugoslavs come from a country where legislation concerning women is more advanced than in the immigration countries. Yugoslav women have in principle already enjoyed many of the conditions regarded, rightly or wrongly, as a possible (or impossible) consequence of migration: notably fertility control and access to paid employment. But the case of the Yugoslavs points at the same time, to the variety of the possible pre-emigration experiences of migrant women in general. For each of them migration represents a very different experience and therefore has a different impact. A minority of Yugoslavs may indeed enter the migration process from a situation of unchallenged values and a rigid observance of 'tradition' may even be strengthened. But most Yugoslavs, and the majority of migrant women in general, do not fit into this 'immobile' profile. For them, emigration is an important step in the process of change already in progress in their own country. The change that takes place during the stay abroad should therefore be seen rather as a continuation of a trend initiated before emigration and as a consequence of the interaction between the migratory and the background influences. As far as Yugoslavs are concerned then, the most important aspects of migration abroad were planned access to paid employment and the intended withdrawal from old social controls. Therefore migration appears as a substitute for a struggle for better conditions and against oppression. Their socialist egalitarian background does not shelter them from oppression and discrimination, but only gives them more strength to fight against it once they have stopped accepting it as normal and natural. The data suggest that in the case of the Yugoslavs at least being a wage earner is a strong card in the hand which puts women in a more powerful position in situations of conflict and opens up more options to

them. It is a condition sine qua non of questioning at least
some dimensions of their subordination. Paid work also
offers a potential for mobilising and organising. Whether
and how women will use it to their own advantage depends
very much both on their background and on their experiences
abroad in which isolation and other forces tend to preserve
their subordinate status and only transform its content -
when they are wage-earners. Migration is not an open door
to emancipation, whatever may be understood by that term.

FEMALE MIGRATION: PERSONAL MOTIVATION OR SOCIO-ECONOMIC PRESSURES

Basically two kinds of explanations for women's presence in
migratory movements are generally put forward, depending
on the author's basic approach: most often, female migration
is explained in terms of individual motives and personal
drives. Seldom is it interpreted in terms of structural
factors and social forces that are seen either as incorporating
these individual motivations or are mentioned independently
from them.

To an individual migrant, her or his decision to emigrate
may appear as her/his own or influenced by another individual. Emigration appears as an individualised act in answer
to the inevitable question of the interviewer: Why did you
leave? But whatever migrants may answer to that question,
the individual motives for emigration are of poor explanatory
value in relation to the migratory process as a whole. These
answers have nevertheless played a central role in many
studies on migration and have served as a basis for endless
typologies and categorisations. This is particularly so in the
case of the migration of women.

Leonetti and Levi (1979) analysed various forms of sociocul-
tural integration of immigrant women into French society.
The essential explanatory variable is a 'person's emigration
project'. The resulting typology (enforced project, economic
project, promotional project, installation project and return
project) serves as a guideline to the author's explanation of
various types of integration (insertion). These typologies
are however unrelated to a broader explanatory framework of
migration. Had the authors done so, the boundaries between
their types would have had to disappear, whatever migrants
say about them or however they qualify their 'projects'. In
this study individual decisions take precedence over other
factors. Individual women appear as free choosers and decision-makers or as those who only follow decisions of another
individual (in the enforced project). The social constraints
on individual decision-making are ignored.

This goes in harmony with the view that migrant women are
social actors, a view that Esthelie Smith (1980) pushes to an

extreme so that the migratory process becomes an arrangement between individuals who are all equally powerful social
actors. Again in opposition to the biased image of women as
followers of men in migration, Thadani and Todaro (1978)
propose a model of migration for 'unattached females' in
developing countries. While initially they acknowledge the
greater importance of structural rather than individual
factors in the migratory process (p. 1) the authors nevertheless seem to give primacy to the latter. 'Particular motivations of female migrants are the individual traits and desires'
(ibid., p. 1), again attributing considerable autonomy to personal and psychological motivations.

While emigration may be an individualised act, it cannot be
explained as a matter of individual motivation, though many
studies have tried to explain migration in those terms.
Whether the individual women appear as free choosers and
decision-makers as Smith tried to convey, or as passive followers of men, the social constraints on the individual deci-
sion-maker must not be ignored. The subjective elements of
migration whether they concern males or females, must be
assessed within the framework of social forces and structural
conditions both in the areas of emigration and immigration,
and not be treated as separate and parallel factors. As
Allen puts it:
  Each individual has reasons for migrating or staying at
  home, but to interpret migration processes on a personal
  basis is to treat the individual as an entity autonomous from
  social forces and thus fail to confront the structure and
  process of migration (1971, p. 29).
Allen has more recently argued that:
  migration of women to Britain has been largely a forced
  migration, both in terms of the structures of dependency
  and in terms of the economic and political relations between
  the Third World and the Metropolitan Centres (1979, p. 29).
It is clear from Arondo's (1975) autobiographical account
that emigration for Maria, a Spanish maid in Paris, was not a
personal decision. The most decisive aspects of female emigration appear in her account: conditions leading to girls'
redundancy in the area, constraints - economic and cultural -
on access to employment locally, a specific labour demand in
the metropolis, and within that context, the patriarchal family
structure, in which the father makes a decision for a girl to
leave.

Abadan-Unat's observation on Turkish female emigration confirms this view about forced migration in terms of dependency
structures within the family (1977). The evidence from the
study of Yugoslav women suggests (Morokvasic, 1980 and
forthcoming) that some common explanations for migrant
women's migration in terms of traditional constraints, migratory policies and, above all, individual motives are inadequate.
The author distinguishes and analyses two sets of determinants

which have an impact on the emigration of women: labour
demand in the immigration countries and a specific position of
women in the spheres of social production and reproduction
in the areas of emigration.   With respect to these latter set
of factors, the author argues that the so-called individual
motives for migration should be reappraised in that context.
These motives often ordinarily indicate nothing more than a
willingness to escape a sexist oppression in the area of
origin.

> What normally is termed 'individual drive' or 'personal
> reason for emigration' related in most cases to the oppres-
> sive and discriminatory nature of the society regarding
> women in the emigration areas (ibid., 1980, p. 56).

The author also draws attention to the statistical evidence
that migrant women by far outnumber men in the category of
widowed, separated or divorced persons ('Labour Supply and
Migration in Europe', 1979; Palmer, 1979).   This evidence
too must be related to the particular status of these women
living as 'manless' and 'family-less' persons in the emigration
areas.   It means that a woman either finds it more difficult
than a man to survive economically while retaining that status
without moving from the area or she finds it more difficult
than a man to change that status within the community, i.e.
remarry (Morokvasic, 1980, p. 55).

Various studies directly or indirectly confirm this: for
example, Macek and Mayer (1972, p. 49) and Andezian and
Streiff (1981, though it is relegated to a footnote).   The
magnitude of this type of emigration as directly influenced by
sexist oppression of the sending societies, and deserving only
a footnote, has yet to be highlighted.

For Arizpe (1980), patterns of male and female migration are
quite different and must be explained in terms of their immediate social context, i.e. community and the household.
Labour demand in the places of destination largely determines
the sex selective patterns.   The cities in Latin America and
in many Asian countries provided opportunities for women to
work as domestic servants so that there has been a tendency
for higher female than male out-emigration.   Who the women
are that migrate can be understood only with reference to the
unequal incorporation of domestic communities into the capitalist sector.   Thus out-migration of females of a certain age
group may be a strategy for survivial for a peasant household who expects her to send remittances for agricultural
inputs and ever greater consumption.   The high rate of out-
migration in female-headed households is explained by discrimination and inequality in the access of women to resources in
the changing peasant economy.   With the latter argument in
mind, it is not clear why Arizpe insists on calling the causes
of emigration, individual motives shared by women of a certain
category.

Young (1980) has a similar approach.   Her research focuses

on the differential out-migration patterns of men and women
in one area of Mexico. Young analyses the structural conditions which allow young girls to be extracted from the rural
areas at an age when they have little knowledge about themselves or alternatives to a life of dependence (Young, 1980,
p. 27). The reasons for the particular composition of the
migration flow are analysed both in terms of the sexual division of labour in the rural areas and the demand for female
labour in the urban area. The author discusses changes
that occurred in the local economy over a period of forty
years and which led to the creation of a relative surplus
population. These changes, as the author argues, were not
primarily set off by the modernisation of agriculture, but by
the monetisation of the local economy, introduction of factory-
produced goods and the destruction of any non-agricultural
domestic manufacturing. This situation created a pressure
to keep young men at home - they were useful in agriculture
(and there was little demand for them in the urban cities) -
and to send young girls away. The girls became redundant
in the village household while at the same time gainful
employment in the cities was readily available to them.

CONCLUDING REMARKS

This discussion represents an attempt to evaluate the differing perspectives which have been brought to bear on the
study of migrant women through varying stages of their
becoming 'visible'.
Each work that I have selected for consideration represents
a contribution to our knowledge of the position of migrant
women and the migratory process as a whole. Many of these
works, particularly in the early period, deserve a highly
critical evaluation. Nevertheless they served a useful function in either stimulating or provoking further research.
But what remains abundantly clear is that the sharing of an
accumulated knowledge in this field, particularly beyond
national boundaries, is still extremely limited. One continues
to find researchers initiating and producing studies in ignor-
ance of similar work in other countries. This not only limits
the potential advances that can be made in this field, it also
encourages the type of ethnocentrism which characterises
much of the literature. There is a continuing sense of déjà
vu as one is confronted by the results of supposedly 'new'
contributions to this literature.
My main aim in this text has been to contribute to an exchange of knowledge, to alert the reader to the theoretical
perspectives and the immense amount of accumulated knowledge which already exists. Hopefully new research will be
guided by such considerations and constitute a real advance
in this field.

2 Motherhood and waged work: West Indian, Asian and white mothers compared

Karen Stone

Irrespective of ethnic origin women wage workers in Britain suffer a similar experience of gender subordination which is the result of sexual divisions within the labour market and the fact that, in addition to their role as economic producers, women are expected to perform the essential role of reproducing and maintaining labour power. Women wage workers, of all ethnic origins, are concentrated in low paid, low status and gender specific employment and the degree of occupational crowding and disparities of job levels and earnings between men and women in Britain are generally much greater than any differences between women of different ethnic origins. However, despite shared characteristics, West Indian, Asian and white female wage-workers in Britain differ both in the proportion who are economically active and in the type of work performed.

This chapter will assess the main similarities and differences in the employment position of the three groups of women and will consider the effects of gender and racial oppression, alongside other factors. Thus in the first section I will compare the economic activity rates and hours of work of women of differing ethnic origin, and question whether differences can be explained solely in terms of economic factors or whether other factors, including differences in the interpretation of gender roles between ethnic groups must be considered. Secondly, I will examine the type of work performed by West Indian, Asian and white women and consider the extent to which objective reasons for their subordinate position in the labour market are viewed as constraints by the women themselves. I consider the extent to which racial categorisation and cultural difference act as an additional constraint on the black women's employment opportunities. In this analysis I will draw on existing literature but will concentrate on my own research which was conducted during 1978 and 1979 in the Handsworth area of Birmingham. This consists of a study of child care facilities; a survey of local employment opportunities; (1) and semi-structured taped interviews with thirty-one West Indian, twenty-two Asian and sixteen white mothers. All the interviews with the mothers were conducted in the home of the respondent and the length of the interview varied from one to five hours. The women were selected from a larger quota sample employed by Rex and Tomlinson in their 1976 survey (Rex and Tomlinson, 1979);

the majority were aged between twenty-four and thirty-five
and all had at least one child aged six years or younger.
All the Asian women interviewed were married, just over half
of the West Indian respondents were married, while just over
a quarter were single and living alone, and 62 per cent of
the white mothers were married.

The majority of the white respondents were born in Britain,
while most of the West Indian women had migrated from
Jamaica.   While Sikhs from India were predominant in the
Asian sample, six of the Asian women were Moslem, five from
Pakistan and one from India.   Just over half (seventeen) of
the West Indian respondents had completed their education in
the West Indies, the majority having left school aged sixteen
or below and twenty-six had no recognised school or occupational qualification.   Similarly most (thirteen) of the white
respondents had left school aged under seventeen but, unlike
the West Indian mothers, nearly half (seven) had a recognised
qualification.   Seven of the Asian women interviewed had
attended school in Britain, eight had been to school in India
or Pakistan for a period ranging from three to twelve years
and seven (four Moslem) of the Asian respondents had never
received any formal education.   One Asian respondent had a
recognised qualification.

None of the Asian respondents had engaged in wage work
prior to migration and of the seventeen West Indian women in
the survey, who were living in the West Indies at an age
when they could have been working, only six had worked outside the home. (2)   Dressmaking, hairdressing, laundry
work, shop work, child care and domestic labour were the
jobs performed by the respondents who were employed in the
West Indies.   Since migration, however, many of the black
women who had not previously engaged in wage labour have
worked.

At the time of the 1978 interviews twenty-one of the thirty-
one West Indian respondents were employed outside the home;
eleven worked full-time and ten part-time.   Of the ten unemployed West Indian women interviewed all said they would like
to work and, indeed, all but two (sisters aged eighteen and
twenty-one) had worked since migration and twenty-eight of
the West Indian respondents had worked outside the home
while they had children below school age.   Although none of
the Asian respondents had been employed prior to migration
nine had engaged in economic activity in Britain.   Five of
these respondents had only worked outside the home (all had
been employed full-time) while four had performed wage work
both in factories and at home.   At the time of the interviews
seven of the Asian respondents were engaged in economic
activity although only three of these women were working outside the home.   An additional eight Asian women said they
would like to work.   Although all sixteen of the white respondents had at some stage engaged in wage work the empha-

sis was on part-time, rather than full-time, work since having children. Indeed in 1978 only seven of the white respondents were employed and all worked part-time.

The high rate of economic activity among the West Indian women interviewed, compared with the white and Asian respondents, is consistent with earlier findings. Thus, in his report of the national PEP study, Smith shows that 74 per cent of the West Indian women surveyed were working compared with 45 per cent of women generally (1977, p. 65). Moreover other studies have shown an even larger discrepancy if analysis is confined to mothers of young children (Hood, 1970; Gregory, 1969 and Pollack, 1972). Among Asian women, on the other hand, Smith found that while non-Moslem Asian women have approximately the same economic activity rates as women generally (45 per cent compared with 43 per cent) the proportion of Moslem Asian women who are engaged in wage labour is substantially lower than the general population (17 per cent - 1977, p. 66).

Moreover, in addition to experiencing different rates of economic activity, the greater emphasis on full-time work amongst the West Indian and Asian women I interviewed, compared with the white respondents, is also supported by other surveys. According to the General Household Survey 90 per cent of non-Moslem Asian women, 75 per cent of Moslem and West Indian working women are employed full-time compared with 60 per cent of all working women in Britain (Smith, 1977, p. 67). Similarly, in her analysis of the 1971 census data for four local authorities, Lomas found that over two-thirds of West Indian and Asian employed mothers of pre-school children were working full-time compared to less than one-third of employed white mothers (1975).

The most obvious explanation as to why women work is because of economic necessity. In the case of West Indian women this is borne out by a number of studies (1974/5 Thomas Coram Research Unit Data reported in Fonda and Moss, 1976; Gregory, 1969 and Lozells Social Development Centre, 1975). Similarly, among Asian women, Wilson found that the women she spoke to 'were almost always subsidiary wage earners; the money they brought in was essential but was not the main wage of the family' (1978, p. 43), and a report on Asian families in Southall argues that 'the high rents and cost of living necessitates that most households have two breadwinners' ('Spare Rib', 1973, p. 17). Also, the desire to purchase a house or return to India or Pakistan may be an important reason why Asian men initially encouraged their wives to work (Sharma, 1971; Wilson, 1978 and Anwar, 1979). In his study of Pakistanis in Rochdale, Anwar also suggests that Pakistani women were motivated to earn a wage so that their husbands could work shorter hours and particularly avoid night-shift work which made the family and social life difficult (1979, p. 134).

Since the wage is such an important reason why women
work an analysis of the economic circumstances of West
Indian, white and Asian families may help to explain why the
three groups of women experience different rates of economic
activity.   Certainly the evidence shows that the economic
circumstances of West Indian and Asian households are less
favourable than those of whites.   At times of high unemployment minority men suffer a disproportionately high rate
of unemployment.   And when in a job minority men earn
less than white men (Smith, 1977).   In addition the financial commitments of West Indian and Asian men are frequently
higher since West Indian and Asian families often have to pay
more for inferior accommodation (Smith, 1977, p. 242, and
Deakin, 1970, p. 86);   the ratio of dependants to working
adults is higher in West Indian and Asian households than in
white, and minority families frequently have financial obligations to family members in their country of origin (Davison,
1968;   Bayliss and Coates, 1965, and Anwar, 1979).   This
evidence would support the argument that a higher proportion of West Indian than white women are engaged in wage
work because of financial necessity, in that the economic circumstances of West Indian families are less favourable than
those of whites.   However, Pakistani families would benefit
most from a wife's wage and yet a smaller proportion of Moslem
women are employed outside the home than either white, West
Indian or Indian women.   Similarly, amongst my sample,
there is no correlation between male earnings and female
employment among the different ethnic groups.

While accepting that women, like men, ultimately work for
the wage, and that women's wages are an essential part of
the economy of many households, I would argue that other
factors also influence whether or not a woman engages in
wage work.   Indeed, since a woman's primary role is defined,
according to dominant ideology, as within the home, mothers
may find it more acceptable to explain their wage work in
terms of the benefits it confers on the family rather than in
terms of the satisfaction that they themselves experience
through employment.   Consequently, surveys which ask
mothers blunt questions about why they work may get a less
than accurate picture of a mother's feelings.   Moreover, even
if it is accepted that women do simply work for the money
provided by employment this in itself can have different implications.   For example, to help relieve the husband's responsibility as breadwinner and/or to provide the woman with a
degree of financial independence.   Certainly the women I
interviewed perceived a woman's wage in very different ways.

As noted earlier, there has been a marked increase in economic activity since migration amongst the West Indian women
I interviewed and it is likely that this can be explained in
terms of the increased availability of regular waged work,
denied them in the West Indies (Foner, 1975).   Certainly the

West Indian women in my sample, as those interviewed by
Foner, valued the greater opportunity for a regular weekly
wage, and thus financial independence, in Britain.

Twenty-nine of the thirty-one West Indian respondents
thought it important for a wife (or cohabitee) to have money
that she has earned herself. A minority of these women felt
that a wife's earnings are important because one wage is not
sufficient, but for the majority financial independence meant
not having to rely on their husband/cohabitee. When asked:
'Do you think it's important for a wife, or a woman living
with a man, to have money she has earned herself?', one
woman explained:

'Yes, because you've got more independence that way, you
know, and you've got your own money coming in just in
case your husband don't feel like giving you any money.
You can tell him what to do with his money and you know
you've got your own in your pocket and you can go and
spend it yourself.'

This sentiment was echoed time and again by the West Indian
women interviewed - they want their own money to buy what
they want without having to ask permission or depend on the
whim of a provider. Although a substantial proportion of the
women's wages was in fact spent on the household, the women
strongly valued the financial control provided by the wage in
that they had a degree of choice over what they purchased.
The majority of working West Indian respondents had not told
their husbands how much they earned and just under half of
the married women questioned did not know their husband's
earnings.

The emphasis placed by the West Indian respondents on the
value of a woman's wage in terms of the financial independence
it provides, and the maintenance of separate, rather than
shared, finances between husband and wife is in sharp contrast to the attitude expressed by the white respondents.
When asked whether they felt it is important for a wife (or cohabitee) to have money that she has earned herself seven of
the white respondents did not think it important because
couples should share their money. A further five respondents thought it important for a wife to earn a wage because
then she could contribute to the household economy, but here
again the emphasis was on sharing. Two of the white women
interviewed thought it depended on the husband's attitude -
whether or not he willingly gives his wife sufficient housekeeping money. Indeed, unlike the West Indian respondents, the
vast majority of the white women interviewed knew how much
their husbands earned and received a regular housekeeping
allowance or shared a bank account with their husband. The
majority of white respondents, therefore, had at least a limited
control over some of the family income even if this involved no
more than deciding what food to buy. This contrasts with
the situation of many of the Asian women I interviewed.

Only three of the Asian respondents receive a regular
housekeeping allowance from their husbands. In four households the husband buys all the food, etc., and only gives his
wife 'pocket money', in three families the woman has to ask
for money, and in another three cases (extended families)
household earnings are pooled and controlled by the parents-
in-law. Of the remaining respondents two households save
the husband's wage and spend the wife's, and in three families the husband gives his wife all his wages and then takes
back what he needs. Thus a large percentage of the Asian
women interviewed did not have control over any money and
yet only one respondent saw the opportunity of a degree of
financial independence provided by a wage as a motive for
working. A woman's wage was perceived by the majority of
Asian respondents as an essential contribution to the household income and of the seven women working at the time of
the interview four said they would not work if their husband
earned sufficient to support the family. However, of these
four, three of the women worked at home and although they
would give up their current work they would nevertheless
like to work outside the home even if it was not financially
necessary:

'I do really like working outside, you know.... At home
you're just by yourself and you're stuck. Outside you
meet more people. You enjoy yourself more. You go out
and you get fresh air and you meet so many people, you
know, and you enjoy it.' (homeworker)

Similarly, the three Asian respondents who said they would
continue to work even if their husband earned sufficient to
support the family, and the eight women who did not work but
would like a job, all explained their reasons for working in
terms of a job providing a relief from the boredom and isolation of domesticity:

'all I know is that I want to work - just go out and do something, anything so long as you're out of the house. You
get so bored, homesick, doing the same job all the time.'
(not working)

Thus, although the majority of the working Asian women interviewed had to work because their wage is an essential contribution to the household income six of the seven employed respondents said they would like to work outside the home, even
if it was not economically essential, because work offers companionship and a relief from the isolation and monotony of
domestic labour. Similarly, when the West Indian respondents
were asked whether they would continue to work outside the
home if their husband earned sufficient money to support the
family, or if social security payments were adequate, fourteen
of the twenty-one working respondents said they would continue working the same hours as present, five would cut their
hours and two did not know how they would react. Only two
of the white working respondents said they would give up

work if it was not financially necessary.   Again the respondents valued work because it provides a relief from the tedium
and isolation of domestic labour and child care:
   'It's not for the money but you get bored being at home....
   I used to clean the house over and over again, you know,
   everything was spotless and I used to do all myself up for
   him coming home from work in the evening and I get sick of
   it' (laughs). (working full-time, West Indian)
The same sentiment was expressed by unemployed women;
   (Why do you want to work?)   'Well because I'm absolutely
   bored to death with staying at home.'   (Do you miss the
   money?)   'No.   No actually the money isn't desperately
   important to me now.   It's just that I need someone to talk
   to now.... I feel depressed.   Well I think it's depressed
   but I've been told that it's not, it's one of them things.   I
   feel lonely and depressed.' (not working, white)
The strong desire expressed by the respondents for friendship and communication is emphasised by their limited social
contacts outside of a work environment.   Those respondents
who were not working outside the home often felt very lonely
and isolated during the day, and amongst all respondents,
both working and unemployed, few went out other than 'occa-
sionally' in the evenings.   Moreover, the isolated situation of
the women was frequently contrasted with the social life of
their husbands.   It was often stated that while men can go
out as they please women need their husband's/boyfriend's
permission and, besides, women are considered responsible for
child care:
   (Do you go out in the evenings?)   'No never.'   (Does your
   husband go out at all?)   'Oh yeh every night....'   (How
   do you think he would react if you went out?)   'Oh stars!'
   (Would he not look after the children?)   'Would he hell.
   No. No - that's what I mean they've got too much - too
   much of their own way.' (white)
and another:
   'I only go out for shopping.   Otherwise it's very hard for
   me cos there's no-one to look after the children.'   (Does
   your husband go out much?)   'He's always out.' (Asian)
Thus among respondents of all ethnic origins work outside
the home was valued because it offers contact with people and
relief from the boredom and isolation of domesticity.   This
need for the companionship provided by working may be made
more necessary by the fact that the women interviewed rarely
socialise in the evenings because of various restraints which do
not apply to their husbands/cohabitees who are free to go out
when they desire.   Also, an obviously crucial motivation to
work is the wage but this was perceived in different terms by
the women interviewed.   While the white and Asian women
tended to value a woman's wage as an essential contribution to
the household economy, it was valued by a majority of the
West Indian women because it provides the woman with a

degree of financial control.   Moreover, the attitude of the
respondents to wage work and their perception of a woman's
wage was related to their definition of the role of women and
their position within the family.

In response to questions about the respective roles of men
and women and the desired characteristics of a husband and
wife it was found that the majority of Asian respondents
were of the opinion that men are 'naturally' more capable outside the home, whereas women excel in the domestic sphere.
Thus a 'good' husband was defined by the Asian women as
one who fulfils the role of economic provider and the Asian
respondents did not expect their husbands to participate in
domestic labour.   Only three characteristics of a 'good' wife
were mentioned: a wife's responsibility to look after the home
and family (mentioned by eleven respondents), obey her husband (six respondents) and obey her in-laws (three respondents):

'We always obey our families, look after the children properly, and good with our relations.   The man should work.'
The majority of the Asian respondents thus accepted rigid sex
role divisions and for many of the Asian women interviewed
(particularly the Moslem respondents) work outside the home
was simply not considered as a possibility for them:

(Why have you never worked?)   'Pakistani women don't do
   it.   We don't work.   We just look after the house.   What
   is a man for?   My husband would not let me work.'
(Husband speaking) 'Work is the man, she has quite a lot
   of job at home - to clean the house, look after the children,
   wash the clothes.' (Moslem)
Moreover the belief that it is a wife's duty to obey her husband and in-laws is going to mean that their opinion will have
a significant influence on a woman's decision to work.   Thus
many of the Asian women were prevented from working or
restricted in their choice of employment, by family constraints.

Unlike the situation which exists among Asian women, where
the decision to work is not the woman's alone but is taken
within the wider context of the family and community, amongst
the West Indian women I interviewed the decision to work was
largely uninfluenced by the opinions of others.

The contrast in attitude between the West Indian and Asian
women is related to their different cultural and religious backgrounds.   Thus while Asian women are traditionally under
the authority of men, who in turn are 'subject to the power
of the elders (both male and female) and the authoritarian
nature of the society as a whole' (Saifullah-Khan, 1976, p.
240), West Indian women have traditionally had to work to
support themselves and their children because West Indian
men have historically been denied fulfilling the role of provider.   Certainly amongst the West Indian respondents there
was not a rigid acceptance of traditional sex role divisions.
Thus nearly three-quarters of the West Indian respondents

expressed the opinion that neither sex has a 'natural' or 'instinctive' ability for particular tasks:
'Well, the men supposed to be stronger and all that non-sense - I don't believe in it.   I think women can do it.... When people say women can't do this you'd be suprised.... They just assume that woman is usually the weaker sex. I've seen it happen that woman isn't always the weaker sex, which is something I know...you know it's just a question of trying to get them to do that and believe that.'
Although the majority of West Indian respondents were of the opinion that a husband should share the domestic labour equally with his wife, however, opposition was expressed in common with the white respondents about the idea of role reversal.   Nevertheless a sizeable minority of both West Indian and white women explained this opposition in economic terms: that men earn more than women and that it therefore made more sense for the man to work for wages.
On the subject of the attributes of a 'good' wife about half the white women interviewed mentioned similar characteristics to those stated by the Asian respondents.   This does not necessarily signify a similarity of attitude, however, since whereas the Asian respondents seemed to accept society's definition of their role a number of the white women, as with the West Indian respondents, recognised the societal definition of a 'good' wife but indicated a certain dissatisfaction with this definition:
'As a wife you're sort of property aren't you?...you've got to do what you're told and you've got to be there when they want you, you've got to explain yourself, anything you do.'
and another:
'They want their wives to be slaves (laughs)...Well I know how he'd like me to be - an old woman (laughs)...just keep the house tidy and things like that.'
Turning now to the respondents' perception of the role of a 'good' mother and of an ideal childhood there was again diversity of opinion amongst the three groups of women interviewed and this is likely to influence the women's attitude to child care and waged work.
While nineteen of the twenty-two Asian women questioned, and fourteen of the sixteen white respondents, thought that the biological mother is always the best person to care for a pre-school child only half of the West Indian women interviewed were of this opinion.   Moreover, whereas all the Asian mothers believed that a mother should devote her life to her children this only applied to two of the white respondents and four of the West Indian women.   Similarly in response to a question about whether the first five years of a child's life are especially significant for the subsequent development of the child opinions differed: whereas seven of the sixteen white respondents were adamant that the first five years are

crucial, and only two of the white women rejected this suggestion, only a small minority of the West Indian (5/31) and
Asian respondents agreed with this notion. Again the diversity of opinion reflects the different cultural backgrounds of
the women. Thus the belief among the white respondents
that the first five years of a child's life are crucial is related
to the ideology of maternal deprivation which has, and continues to be, used to justify inadequate child-care provision
in Britain, and whereas it is believed within Asian and white
society that pre-school children should be cared for by their
biological mother or close relatives, child care in the West
Indies tends to be shared.

Thus while the incentive of a wage is obviously an important
reason why women work I would argue that it is not the only
factor to be considered and the different employment rates
among West Indian, Asian and white women cannot be understood simply in terms of financial need. Thus neither
nationally, nor within my sample, is there a correlation
between male earnings and female employment rates among the
different ethnic groups. Also, a majority of the women I
interviewed said that they would continue to work outside the
home even if it was not financially necessary. All three
ethnic groups valued work for the companionship it provided
and the opportunity to escape from the tedium and isolation of
domestic labour. However while this, together with the
wage, was a shared incentive to work the three different
ethnic groups exhibit different rates of economic activity and
I would argue that differences in the interpretation of gender
roles between the three groups of women must be considered.

Women in the West Indies have little choice about engaging
in wage work when it is available. Slavery and colonialism in
the West Indies meant the creation of societies moulded socially
and economically in the interests of the metropolitan society.
The economic legacy has been underdevelopment, high levels
of unemployment and persistent poverty for the bulk of the
population (Girvan, 1972). Historically, West Indian men
have been denied the opportunity of earning sufficient to
maintain a wife and children. Thus for a woman in the West
Indies the role of motherhood has always included the provision of financial support for her children, the latter's care
shared among female kin, particularly the grandmother (Philpott, 1977). But regular waged work is even more difficult
for women to find than it is for men. Migration provides an
escape route and indeed the migration of West Indian women
has historically responded to employment opportunities (Eisner,
1961, p. 151). Certainly a very strong desire for financial
independence was evident among the women I interviewed and
similar findings have been reported by Foner (1975). The
West Indian respondents, in my survey, made the decision to
work independently of the opinions of others and the tradition
of shared child care amongst West Indian women may make the

decision to work less guilt ridden than among white mothers who subscribe to the notion of maternal deprivation.

The majority of the white respondents, unlike the West Indian women, believed that married couples should share their money and that a woman's wage is important because it is a contribution to the household economy rather than a means of financial independence.   Moreover, child care in white society is defined as the duty of the biological mother and many women who would like to work are often prevented from so doing by a sense of duty to being a full-time house-wife.   Certainly, amongst my sample, the majority of the white respondents felt that the biological mother is always the best person to care for the child and subscribed to the idea that the first five years of a child's life are crucial for its future development.

Asian women share with their West Indian counterparts the same background of British colonialism, but the colonial experience differed in many important respects.   For instance, the imposition of new economic forms did not basically alter the position of women within the social structure (Wilson, 1978).   The role of Asian women is strictly defined as within the family and it is women who take responsibility for the domestic sphere while men are responsible for gaining the livelihood of the household.   Thus amongst my sample only one Asian woman was motivated to work by the opportunity of a degree of financial independence.   In a majority of the Asian households finance was controlled by the husband or in-laws.   Asian culture places considerable emphasis on the importance of the family and on obligations and responsibilities towards family members while individualism is played down. Thus the decision as to whether or not a woman should work is not hers alone but is taken within the wider context of the family and community.   Also, a majority of the Asian respondents felt that a mother should devote her life to her children.

Asian culture defines a woman's role as within the home and wage work among women is thus a break with tradition.   The low wages of Asian men obviously provide an impetus for this break with custom but the different rates of economic activity between Moslem and non-Moslem women illustrates the continuing importance of cultural background and religion.

EMPLOYMENT PATTERN

Of the sixty-nine women I interviewed fifty-four had engaged in economic activity in Britain and in this section I briefly consider the employment pattern of the respondents.   Table 2.1 sets out the jobs held by all employed respondents at the time of interviewing.

TABLE 2.1 *Jobs held by employed respondents at time of interview*

West Indian mothers		White mothers	
Assembler	1	Press operator	1
Packer	1	Packer	1
Setter operator	1	Viewer	1
Jewellery trade	1	Cleaning	2
Sewing trade	1	Catering	1
Cleaning	6	Playgroup	2
Children patrol	1		8
Bingo operative	1		—
National Health Service	6	Asian mothers	
Office	1	Machine operator	1
Catering	1	Sorter	1
	21	Machinist	1
	—	Homework	4
			7
			—

(Note: 1 white respondent was employed part-time as both a cleaner and a cook)

West Indian respondents

The vast majority of West Indian women interviewed were concentrated in unskilled and semi-skilled repetitive factory work
traditionally performed by women.   Only one respondent, a
setter operator, held a skilled factory position and this woman
was the only respondent currently performing work traditionally associated with men.   The average rate of pay of the
respondents was £1.10 an hour (in 1978).

An analysis of work histories shows that pregnancy was the
most common reason given for leaving all jobs held since
migration among the West Indian respondents (23/78) followed
by redundancy or factory closure and nine jobs were resigned
because child-care arrangements had become unsatisfactory.
With the exception of three West Indian respondents who had
remained at their jobs for over six years the average length
of employment, without a break, at the same firm was twenty-
one months.

Seventeen per cent of all jobs held by the West Indian respondents were with the National Health Service while the

corresponding figure for the white interviewees was 7 per
cent.   Figures for the country as a whole show that immigrant women are concentrated in the least desirable and
lowest status areas of the NHS (Department of Employment,
1976).

White respondents

All of the sixteen white respondents had at some stage engaged in wage work although since having children the
emphasis was on part-time, rather than full-time, employment
and all seven women employed at the time of the interview
worked part-time.   Like the West Indian, the white respondents were concentrated in traditionally female occupations,
over one-third were engaged in unskilled or semi-skilled
factory work, and the average hourly rate of pay of the
white women was almost the same as the West Indian respondents (£1.07 an hour).   These common characteristics of
employment shared by white and black women reflect the
national pattern.   Indeed, both D.J. Smith (1977) and
Mayhew and Rosewell (1978) conclude that the difference in
job levels between men and women is more striking than any
difference between women of different ethnic origins.   Similarly Smith found that within the job levels occuped by women
there were no disparities of earnings between white and black
women (1977, p. 87), and Bayliss and Coates show that the
take-home pay of the West Indian and white women interviewed
was 'fairly similar' while there was a large difference between
the pay of West Indian and white men (1965, p. 163).
Unlike the West Indian respondents, however, over half the
jobs held by the white women interviewed were in the service,
distribution and office sectors.   Thus although both the
white and black respondents were concentrated in traditionally
female occupations the white women were over-represented in
shop and office work while the West Indian women were over-
represented in the NHS.   Again this reflects the situation
nationally (Mayhew and Rosewell, 1978).
The average number of jobs held by each of the white respondents was four and they left jobs on average after eighteen
months.   As with the West Indian respondents the most frequent reason for leaving a firm was pregnancy but the second
most common reason was that the woman obtained a higher
paid job (eight).

Asian respondents

The employment pattern of the Asian respondents differs significantly from that of the West Indian and white women interviewed.   Less than half (nine/twenty-two) of the Asian

respondents had ever been engaged in economic activity, they had only held a total of eighteen jobs between them, and had stayed an average of three years in each job.   Of the reasons given for leaving particular jobs pregnancy was the most common (four) but marriage was also a frequent reason (three).   Unlike the West Indian and white women interviewed homework was fairly common amongst the Asian respondents.

At the time of the interviews three of the Asian women were engaged in low paid factory work, and four were employed as homeworkers;   Mrs Singh sews trousers at home, she is paid 20p a pair and it takes her half an hour to make a pair of trousers if she is not interrupted.   The work arrives spasmodically.   The respondent (in common with the other three homeworkers) bought her own sewing machine and does not receive any holiday or sick pay.   She was anxious to know 'what are you going to do with this information' and she would prefer to work in a factory:

'because at home you're just by yourself and you're stuck. ... At home you can't work with the children because when they start crying and that you stop, you know, and you get sort of confused.   When you're at home you've got your housework to do as well as your work.   You've got to work hard by yourself doing overtime.'

CONSTRAINTS ON EMPLOYMENT OPPORTUNITIES

Despite differences in the employment patterns of the West Indian, Asian and white mothers interviewed the jobs held by the vast majority were low status, badly paid, semi-skilled or unskilled and repetitive.   As to why the respondents are concentrated in low-level jobs several factors appear relevant.

An obvious similarity in the work performed by the three groups of women is that the jobs held by both the black and white women are jobs traditionally defined as 'women's work'. There are rigid sexual divisions within the labour market and those jobs which are defined as 'women's work' invariably command lower rates of pay, status and skill.   Higher paid skilled jobs tend to be the preserve of men.   However, when the respondents were asked whether they had ever been rejected for a job because of their sex only three white women replied in the affirmative.   The most frequent response to the question was 'I've never applied for a job that a man would do' and this confirms the results of an employment survey I undertook in May 1978.

The results of this survey indicated that both applicants for jobs and employers are aware that some jobs are 'women's work' and are prepared to accept rigid sexual divisions. Thus of the 159 applicants for office work only seven were men.   Similarly of the fifty-three applicants for shop jobs

three were men, and only six men were included in the 121
applicants for cleaning jobs.   In the case of a vacancy for a
'B/Operative' apparently a few men applied not realising the
abbreviation stood for 'Bingo' and 'when you get men who
ring up, when they find out what it is they usually say "oh,
it's women that do that sort of work" and ring off.'   Similarly, the three men who telephoned in response to an advertisement for a Hand and Power Press Operator probably did
not realise that according to the employer, 'women are better
workers on hand and power press because of aptitude....
They are quick and get a hold of boring jobs' and therefore
men would only be appointed if there were no suitable female
applicants.   Obviously the situation exists in reverse and
when I inquired whether a firm had received any female applicants in response to an advertisement for Stampers I was told
'It's a man's job.'
Since there is this selection process at the job application
stage it comes as little surprise to find that in the actual factory situation women do the 'repetitive and boring' jobs.
Women are the machinists, assemblers, viewers, clerk typists,
etc.
During the interviews, in which I also questioned the employers about their policy and attitude towards West Indian
and Asian workers, the Personnel Officers seemed comfortable
about making blatantly sexist statements whereas they were
extremely concerned about any comments which could indicate
racial discrimination.   Thus, when asked why certain jobs
are 'women's work' employers frequently resorted to naturalis-
tic explanations, for example 'women are more nimble', 'tend
to be more patient', 'the bottle neck jobs are done by men
because they need physical strength.'   Similarly, one Personnel Officer was adamant that the division between those
people who could be trained as skilled engineers and those
who could not fell along sexual lines: 'Women don't have an
engineering attitude of mind, not engineering minded...men
can be trained to do housework but you have to change attitudes.'   The assumption that a woman is a man's dependant
was also strong when a Personnel Officer was explaining that
the men do not apply for the 'women's jobs' because they are
lower paid and 'If a man gets a job he has a certain standard
of living to maintain.   A man earning £50 a week only takes
home about £40.   If a woman comes to work it's £30 extra.'
The existence of rigid divisions in the labour market
between what are defined as 'men's jobs' and 'women's work'
means black and white women share a fundamental discrimination on the grounds of sex.   They are confined, in the main,
to work which is semi- or unskilled and low paid.   Thus even
though the categories of work performed by white women
differ to some extent from that done by black women the
rates of pay are similar.
Women are categorised primarily as actual or potential wives

and mothers and their wage work is considered secondary to
their role as domestic labourers in the home. Child care is
defined as the responsibility of the mother and the ideology
of wage work is in direct opposition to the ideology
of motherhood. Thus many mothers who would like to work
outside the home do not because they feel that their children
need them full-time. This situation applied to nine white
women in my sample and thirteen of the fifteen non-working
Asian respondents said that they would not work while they
had small children. Indeed, in response to the question
'Generally what do you think about mothers with children
under five working - do you think the children suffer?' nine
of the sixteen white and twelve of the thirty-one West Indian
mothers replied in the affirmative, although a few lowered the
age of the child from five to three years. Of the remainder,
two white and ten West Indian women thought that whether or
not the child suffers depends on the mother or the quality of
substitute care, etc., and five white and eight West Indian
mothers did not think the child is disadvantaged by the
mother working. Amongst the Asian respondents one mother
thought 'if a woman is working it's much helpful' and four of
the Asian women interviewed thought it acceptable for the
woman to work if satisfactory child-care arrangements have
been made. Sixteen Asian respondents expressed the opinion
that young children suffer if their mother engages in wage
work. Thus for many women, for them, as mothers, to
engage in economic activity means that they have failed, to
some extent, in their role of mother. Some respondents experienced guilt because they felt children suffer if they are
separated from the mother, other respondents found difficulty
in concentrating on the two roles, others felt that they were
too tired to care for their child adequately while some of the
women interviewed were dissatisfied with the type of child
care available. The following quotes illustrate a few of the
emotional conflicts experienced by working mothers:
  'I think they do suffer (if the mother works) but I don't
  like to talk about that because otherwise I get depressed
  because I think that these children have been deprived, you
  know, because I did go to work. But there again if I did
  stay at home I wouldn't have been a nurse so there's no
  solution. Even if I had another child now I would have to
  figure some way of getting back to work, even if it was
  only part-time. I wouldn't like to give up my job.' (West
  Indian)
and another:
  'At those early stages to leave the children all day, early
  morning till late at night, which was what I did, it was
  wrong.' (white)
Moreover, even if women wage labourers resolve these emotional conflicts they face numerous practical constraints on
working. Indeed the majority of respondents were of the

opinion that having children rather than their sex, membership of a racialised group or lack of qualifications was the
most important restriction on their choice of employment.
Children were seen as a restriction in two major ways.
Firstly the women had found that the majority of employers
question female applicants about their family responsibilities
and appear reluctant to employ a mother of small children:

'The children make it more difficult.   When I applied, when
I was looking for a job, I applied fifteen times.... This one
I have was the sixteenth, you see, and I told them how
many kids I have (four) and they said "how will you cope?"
... So I come home and says "Oh I haven't got the job."
... When you tell them the amount of children you've got
they think well too many children, that one won't be able
to cope.'   (Have you ever gone for a job where they didn't
ask how many children you have?)   'No.   They ask if
you're married and how many kids.' (West Indian)

Secondly, the women are limited to jobs with hours which are
compatible with the hours of their child-care provision:

'Everybody complains it's difficult to get a job but I could
get a job...but it's a matter of whether you have someone
to look after the children.' (West Indian)

'If I hadn't got these [children] I could go full-time and I
could do anything but having to do part-time you're sort of
limited, there's only certain jobs and there's a great rush
for them.' (white)

Both the emotional conflict and practical difficulties experienced by employed mothers of young children are made worse
by the inadequacy of full-time child-care provision.   Thus
many of the women I interviewed who felt guilty about leaving
their children during the day said they would be happier if
they could make a more satisfactory arrangement for child
care;   for many mothers there is simply no choice however.
    Indeed there was a high level of dissatisfaction with the
particular child-care arrangement used by the mothers
although the level of satisfaction with local authority day nurseries and nursery schools was higher than other forms of
provision.   Thus while only one of the fifteen West Indian
mothers whose child/ren had attended a local authority day
nursery was not satisfied, seven of the ten who had employed
child-minders, and five out of the six of those who had used
a split-shift system of child care with their husbands, were
dissatisfied.   Similarly while the two white mothers who had
used a child-minder and a split-shift system were both un-
happy about the arrangement, eight of the eleven using a
local authority day nursery were relatively satisfied.   All the
Asian mothers whose children had attended a nursery school
were pleased with the care that had been provided and particularly the preparation for school that their children had
received.
    The obvious disadvantage of local authority day nurseries,

mentioned by a substantial number of the respondents, is the
expense and the inadequacy of provision. In Birmingham,
since 1 April 1979, all new admissions to day nurseries have
been subjected to a maximum charge of £14 per week. Moreover, the number of places provided is insufficient to meet
demand and in March 1978 there were 714 children on the city
waiting list. Places are allocated according to priority which
is defined as:

children whose admission is urgently required on grounds
such as the break up of the family, illness or confinement
of the mother, medical reasons occasioned by unsatisfactory
housing conditions, or in fact other circumstances as would
justify their admission on social need or for health reasons
(Report of the Director of Social Services, February 1979).

Thus although local authority day nurseries are a preferred
form of provision among my respondents many mothers cannot
obtain a place and/or pay the fees. Consequently mothers
are forced to use a form of provision which they consider less
satisfactory and this is likely to increase the conflict they experience between the roles of wage worker and mother. In
addition, some forms of child-care provision (e.g. nursery
schools and playgroups) operate restricted hours which limit
the mother's choice of employment.

All women wage-workers are restricted in their choice of
employment by rigid sexual divisions within the labour market
and mothers are further restricted because child care is
defined as a mother's responsibility and provision is inadequate. In addition, however, there are a number of factors
which operate to further constrain black women workers.

West Indian and Asian men and women workers tend to be
concentrated in lower level jobs than white workers and, as
Ceri Peach has described, migrants have acted as a replacement population in regions and employment sectors which
could not attract sufficient white workers. Similarly the
main conclusion of more recent studies is that black workers
are regarded as undesirable by many employers who only take
on a black worker when no other labour is available (see
Smith, 1977 and Anwar, 1979). Although the PEP survey
found that discrimination was lower for black women than men
(Smith, 1977, p. 120) the level of discrimination revealed by
correspondence testing was nevertheless high. Certainly,
black women experience a higher rate of unemployment than
white women: 'According to the Census, the level of unemployment among women born in the West Indies, India or Pakistan was 9.3 per cent, compared with 5.6 per cent for all
women in the workforce' (Smith, ibid., p. 72).

It is not surprising, therefore, that while only two white
respondents experienced any difficulty in obtaining work one-
third of the West Indian women interviewed found it difficult
to get a job. Only seven West Indian respondents, however,
felt that they had been rejected for a job simply because they
were black:

'Why I don't get jobs is because of me colour.   Several times I've rung up for a job, been told to come in for an interview and then as soon as they see me they say the job's gone.' (West Indian)

Thus West Indian and Asian women workers in Britain suffer from both sexual and racial oppression but in addition Asian women experience a number of cultural constraints on their employment options.

Jobs which involve contact with unrelated men are unacceptable for Moslem women who adhere to the principles of purdah, and are regarded with suspicion by non-Moslem Asians.   Thus, homework or work in an all female environment is the only option available for many Asian women and, as illustrated by my respondents, the employment conditions of homeworkers are notoriously bad.

Also, work which involves adopting English clothing may be out of the question for many Asian women since traditional forms of dress are an integral part of the purdah system, and for women from India 'such an important part of Indian culture that many women do not take up a job if they are required to accept Western dress' (Uberoi, 1964, p. 35). Furthermore, in addition to preference for a female working environment and ability to wear traditional dress, there may also be restrictions by caste and James argues that more conservative Sikhs consider it improper for a Jat woman to be employed by a person of another caste (1974, p. 91).

Inability to speak English, lack of information and knowledge of rights, and unfamiliarity with a wage economy operate to further restrict Asian women in their choice of employment (Wilson, 1978).   But these factors also restrict Asian women in their *search* for employment and many find work through a friend or relative.   This process tends to exacerbate segregation and may exclude Asian women from more desirable work obtainable through alternative channels.

However, even if Asian women did not experience cultural constraints on their choice of employment, and were familiar with the British labour market, sexual and racial oppression would continue to inhibit their employment options.   Black women suffer from both racial and sexual categorisation. These forms of oppression obviously differ and both must be challenged in order to fight the exploited position of black women.   Black women do experience higher rates of unemployment than white women but in other respects their situation in the British labour market is more similar to white females than black males.   In terms of job levels and earnings the differences between men and women are greater than disparities between women of different ethnic origins.   Thus the employment of the women I interviewed was similar in that they were concentrated in low paid, low status and gender specific work.   Moreover, the three groups of women interviewed shared a similar consciousness in that the majority

identified having children, rather than pure sexual or racial
discrimination, as the major constraint on their employment
options.   The majority recognised, but did not challenge,
rigid sexual divisions within the labour market and only a
small minority of the black women acknowledged personal
racial discrimination.   Despite these similarities, however,
differences between the West Indian, Asian and white respondents were also evident.   Consistent with national statistics
the three groups of women experienced different rates of
economic activity and the differences did not correspond with
differences in the economic circumstances of the families.
Moreover, there was a marked contrast in the way the women
perceived a woman's wage and in family finance organisation
which can only be properly understood with reference to cultural differences in the perception of gender roles and definitions of motherhood.

NOTES
1 Two methods were employed in this survey.   Firstly the
   job columns of the 'Birmingham Evening Mail' were
   scanned every day for two weeks and jobs suitable for
   women in my sample were selected.   Firms which had
   placed the advertisement were then telephoned and asked
   to give an indication of the number of applications which
   had been received and the proportion of male and female
   applicants.
      The second method was to interview the Personnel Offi-
   cers of major firms in the area.
2 The respondents defined 'work' as regular employment and
   it is possible that a larger number of women interviewed
   had worked in irregular jobs which they failed to mention.

3 The second generation: West Indian female school leavers[1]

Shirley Dex

A great deal of research attention has been paid to the position of children of black migrant workers in Britain. (2)
This academic concern has been submerged during the 1980s
by a widespread current of racist belief in British society
which castigates black youth as nothing more than a 'law and
order' problem.   It is worth remarking that, on the whole,
it is not the women who had made 'news'.

The migration (of the first generation) has been given some
examination in the context of the fluctuations of Western capitalist economies (Castles and Kosack, 1973; Peach, 1978/9;
Robinson, 1980; Phizacklea and Miles, 1980), and we can see
from these studies, the significant inter-relationships which
the migration process and the numbers involved has had with
national economic changes, particularly in the post Second
World War period.   More recently attempts have been made
to reverse the migration process in a more permanent fashion,
concomitant with a general decline in Western European national economic prospects (Castles, 1980a).   At the same time,
there is evidence of more sweeping international changes in
the structural balance of the world economy, through the
development of multinational companies and their capital
investment programmes.   (See Mary Hancock's chapter in
this volume.)   Just how and where the second generation
migrants fit into these major and minor structural economic
changes remains to be uncovered.   A start is made on such
a task in this paper by examining the job histories of a group
of second generation women of West Indian parentage.
Women have tended to be ignored so far in other work which
tackles these issues.

Second generation female West Indians in Britain are a
group of black women, described as being 'between two cultures' as a result of the migration process, and yet some of
them have had the largest proportion of their education in
British schools.   They also constitute the beginning of new
kinship relations in Britain, to replace those broken by migration, although this cannot be pursued here.   Moreover, they
are mainly women from working-class backgrounds, their
parents being mainly confined to manual jobs since migration
and having experienced considerable racial discrimination
(Smith, 1977) despite legislation outlawing such practices.
Nevertheless there is always an expectation that the second
generation of any migrant group will attain a more equal

starting point in comparison with the young indigenous population. There are however good reasons to suggest that this
might not be the case from the evidence of underachievement
amongst West Indian school children, although this is the subject of some debate in the case of West Indian women. (3)
The need for an empirical examination of the position of the
second generation young women in labour markets remains
clear and long overdue.

Women workers in Britain have been said to constitute both
a reserve army of labour (Bruegel, 1979 and Beechey, 1978)
and a secondary workforce (in the dual labour market theory;
Barron and Norris, 1976).   Bruegel has demonstrated the
need to tread carefully in using concepts developed primarily
for application to men workers.   These frameworks exist as
heuristic devices for an examination of women workers but it
must be noted that they have not addressed themselves to the
position of black, and/or migrant women as such and we must
beware taking them on in total, in advance of some empirical
examination.   For example, if the three dimensions, of
gender, colour or ethnic origin, and class are examined separately with respect to paid work and jobs, a group of second
generation West Indian women might be expected to score less
than whites along each dimension.   But some of the recent
studies of ethnicity and work   suggest that we should not set
out with the preconceived notion that black working-class
women's status will be doubly or trebly disadvantaged, in an
additive way.   Louden (1978) found, for example, that the
self-esteem of black women can be higher than that of whites.
These matters are problematic, and because individuals can,
and do respond to their circumstances, new outcomes are possible.

This paper sets out to examine a group of second generation
West Indian women in Britain with these issues and concerns
in mind, at the point of their transition from school to work
(and the five years which follow) and in comparison with a
group of similarly educated white women.   We can only begin
to tackle the questions in this paper, and with this data
source.   Since the school-leavers were mostly what we would
call 'working class' the analysis to be undertaken here is
examining 'within-class relations'.   It is inevitable that we
should draw upon other literature which has been concerned
either with the migration process, or the significance of ethnic
origin in the workplace, or with the place of women in labour
markets, but this study seeks to integrate these concerns
rather than treat them as separate issues.

Some of the useful conclusions from these other (partial)
studies are described in the discussion which follows.   The
later sections then describe the data source and examine the
results and conclusions.

THE MIGRATION PROCESS AND WOMEN'S WAGE LABOUR

Aspects of this subject matter have been treated in other
studies, but the whole topic, integrating the migration process, ethnic group employment, women's employment, and then
examining the second generation, has not been tackled in
British research, although more recently, second generation
ethnic minority men's employment has been receiving some
attention (Dex, 1979, 1981).   This is not to say that the
other studies which touch on this subject matter have nothing
to offer;   they do.   There have been some important argu-
ments emerging from these strands which are reviewed in
brief below, and they suggest what the principles and direc-
tions of research should be.
     The topic of women's employment has been receiving in-
creasing attention over the past decade as women have been
seen to be increasingly participating in the formal paid employment sector.   There has not been any consensus, however, on what is the best way to conceptualise women's employment. (4)   The idea of women being a reserve army
(being thrown out and drawn in to wage labour according to
the needs of capital) has received support although it needs
to be qualified and elaborated for women as a whole (Bruegel,
1979) and none of the work in this area considers the position
and problems for theory raised by migrant women (see
Phizacklea's chapter in this volume).   The dual labour
market theory is worth mentioning as a separate development
since, as suggested on the basis of empirical work in American
labour markets, it claimed to describe the position of both
blacks' and women's employment in the secondary sector.
Some British studies have been incorporating this conceptualisation into their research on women's and blacks' employment
(e.g. Barron and Norris, 1976;   Bosanquet and Doeringer,
1973), but it has many drawbacks and it has not been fully
justified as a useful tool for the analysis of British labour
markets (Dex, 1979) although there clearly are aspects of the
theory which are appropriate to the segregation of women's
jobs and earnings opportunities in Britain.
     The dual labour market theory presents a particularly static
view of labour markets, and the way in which the segregation
arises is not made clear.   Neither is the significance of age
and other divisions within the labour force elaborated as far
as the job structures are concerned: for example, should we
expect differences between young and older workers, and
between white and black women, or is their common men's or
women's gender identity the characteristic of overriding importance in allocating them a place in the sectors?   The dual
labour market theory, as outlined so far, is so vague as to be
at best heuristic, and not immediately relevant to the task in
hand.
     Migrant and indigenous women in Britain do share the

experience that they have been drawn in large numbers into the paid employment sector over the same period, and that their children both share the status of being a type of second generation women's labour force. How far this common experience, by virtue of their gender group is reflected in their employment, domestic organisation and other aspects of social life remains to be seen. It does mean, however, that in a comparison between second generation black women and young white women, the white women can act as a type of control group, and the comparison will hopefully begin to identify characteristics which owe their origin to the common identity of women in labour markets from those which have their roots in the migration process and the ethnic status of the groups.

We can divide the migration studies which have relevance to our concern into three groups; those concerned with the migration process, those concerned with the position of migrants in the British economy (race or ethnic relations studies) and in a very few cases, those which attempt to integrate the migration itself, the sending society values and the position of migrants in Britain. Common to all these areas of study is a relative lack of concern with women migrants.

Studies which have examined the migration process (e.g. Nikolinakos, 1975; Bellini, 1974/5; Rees and O'Muirchertaigh, 1976) have been concerned, almost wholly, with the numbers of migrants, failing to distinguish between the sexes or the generations.

But one of the useful questions which emerged from Castles and Kosack's (1973) study of the migration process (although the extent to which it is fully appropriate to migrant women's labour is difficult to tell) is the suggestion that migrant workers occupy a specific subordinate place in the economic structure of advanced capitalist Western European countries, and that this can be thought of as a permanent position for migrant workers, even if the jobs are occupied over time by different migrants. This raises the question of whether or not the second generation will take over their parents' 'migrants' position' in these national economic structures, although we must be careful not to view this as necessarily a static 'position'.

Two problems arise if one tries to answer this question about second generation migrant women's position in the economic structure. We would need to know the position of first generation migrant women and the extent to which their position differs from that of indigenous women and this is poorly documented. Hence, any assessment of whether the second generation continue to fill the same parts of the structure as their mothers is more difficult to answer, because of a lack of information. The second problem arises from the fact that the structure of women's employment has traditionally varied with the age structure, and although this phenomenon also is not fully documented, it seems likely that older women have different types of jobs than younger school-leavers. Thus, any comparison between the first and second generation migrant women and their employment has to reckon with these structural age divisions. Nevertheless, the question raised by Castles and Kosack provides a useful background against which to think of constructing theories about women, employment, the migration process and economic structures.

Of the studies which have focused on the position of migrants in Britain most have one or more shortcomings. The larger surveys (e.g. by the PEP) have paid minimal attention to women and their work, even when they have been incorporated into the samples. Some of the community studies (e.g. Rex and Moore, 1967; Allen et al., 1977; Rex and Tomlinson, 1979) have advocated linking the migration process with migrants' positions but they have not been very successful in achieving their aims. They have also lacked any serious consideration of women's employment.

Work on West Indian life-styles in Britain by Pryce (1978) does try to integrate the background sending society values into his classification of West Indian life-styles in Britain by suggesting that there are structural parallels between the effects of colonialism in the West Indies and the subordinate status of West Indians in Britain. His work does incorporate second generation youths, but it is rather impoverished as far as women are concerned; they are very much a peripheral concern.

A far better attempt to integrate sending and receiving society structures which is one of the few serious pieces of research to focus on West Indian women is by Foner (1979). She suggested that the work of first generation Jamaican migrant women in London had far-reaching consequences on their attitudes, household organisation and relationships in ways which were different from the West Indies. In that she aimed to achieve an ambitious study of comparative social structures, the work is not entirely successful, but it does, like Pryce's work, reveal some of the possibilities for integrating the migration process and women's work in Britain.

Phizacklea (1982) has attempted this next step in analysing the overall position of first generation West Indian migrant women within British labour markets. Taking into account the structural features of West Indian social formations which make the search for waged work *and* therefore migration, an imperative for women, she then goes on to analyse their position within British labour markets. She concludes that West Indian women as a racially and sexually categorised fraction of the working class have taken on, what Castles and Kosack have described, as a 'permanent migrant's position', supplying cheap and flexible labour power. That the majority of women have effectively settled permanently in Britain has done little to change their function within the labour market.

These studies collectively reveal that there are some clear omissions and consequent needs in this general area. The topic of women's employment is one which is problematic, and there has been a tendency towards over-theorising and under-researching. Migrant women have largely been omitted as a serious and heterogenous group by that tradition in Britain. There is, therefore, a clear need for work which links the migration process with the study of women and ethnic relations in Britain. Such studies need to go beyond the correlation of aggregate 'immigrant' numbers with the economic requirements and opportunities of Western capitalist economies to examine the changes which arise, both within and between social group relationships. They also need to allow a place for positive action on the part of the participants (Genovese, 1971; Wallman, 1979). In the labour market, this would mean that both the first, and especially the second generations, were seen as being able to respond to the structure of constraints and opportunities and help to mould them over time.

There are obvious dangers to be avoided in the process of trying to link migration and the sending and receiving society social structures. We must avoid offering values and attitudes, etc. found in the sending society as an explanation of certain behaviour or responses in the metropolitan society, giving them the status of 'West Indian characteristics'. This would be a very incomplete (if not racist) sort of explanation if it did not also include a discussion of why this particular aspect had come to be a significant distinguishing characteristic in the receiving society and why other values or forms of behaviour had declined in importance. By taking a view in which individuals and groups can actively respond and interact with their (new) environment, rather than being a bundle of 'inherent' characteristics, we should be able to guard against such partial, unsociological, and what can easily fall into racist explanations. Then the question can be usefully asked 'Under what circumstances does this phenomenon arise?'

The empirical questions which arise from this discussion and the outline of the general area of need are as follows:

What is the position of second generation West Indian young women in the British economy?

Do West Indian second generation young women occupy, in any sense, a 'permanent' migrant's status or position in the British economy?

Are there any identifiable migrant women's responses to be found as the second generation West Indian young women interact with labour market structures, and if so, under what circumstances do they arise?

Are there other links between the migration process and the position in the economic structure of second generation women, bearing in mind that this can be a changing position?

These questions are used below to organise the presentation
of the results from a secondary analysis of a data source
which is described first.   The questions are thought to form
a good basis for hypothesis and theory construction in this
field, rather than being seen as testing already existing
theories.

THE YOUNG PEOPLE'S EMPLOYMENT STUDY

The extent to which these questions can be answered was set
for the purposes of this paper within the bounds of the available data from a survey of school-leavers in Birmingham and
London commencing in 1971, collected for the Department of
Employment by the Office of Population Censuses and Surveys
(OPCS).   The full details of the sampling procedures are
outlined elsewhere (Sillitoe, 1972, and Dex, 1981) and are
summarised only here.   The main aim in devising this survey
was to compare West Indian migrants' children, who had the
whole or a large part (a complete secondary education) of
their education in British schools, with similarly educated
whites.   White school-leavers were then found to match these
second generation West Indians by having the same age, educational qualifications, sex and where possible, being from the
same class or school. (5)   378 second generation West Indians
and 463 matched whites were interviewed initially.   The
number of whites was greater than the number of West Indians
since a number of white 'reserves' were incorporated who also
were matched to West Indians in the sample.
   The survey was longitudinal and consisted of four interviews with each individual.   There was, as expected, a loss
from the sample as the interviews progressed at intervals of
six months after leaving school, two - fifteen months later,
three - eighteen months later and four - two years later. (6)
At the fourth interview there were 255 West Indians and 324
matched whites left in the sample.   The numbers of young
women used in this analysis who left school in 1971 are outlined in Table 3.1, for the two cities.   Whites who had the
status of being a reserve at either the first or fourth interview were not included in these sub-samples.
   The interviews with each school-leaver provided a job history for those remaining in the sample for all four interviews
which covered the five years after they left school. (7)   The
data collected at each interview was concerned mostly with
employment and unemployment experiences and the attitudes
towards such.   Interviews were also carried out, wherever
possible, with one of the parents, the teacher and with the
Youth Employment Officer, on the basis of the statutory interview held with each child.   The information from these
interviews, for some reason, is very incomplete with large
numbers 'not available'.

TABLE 3.1   *Numbers of female school-leavers used in this analysis from the Young People's Employment Study*

1971 Female school-leavers	Interview February 1972	Interview November 1976
London		
West Indian	67	36
Whites	67	36
Total	134	72
Birmingham		
West Indian	54	38
Whites	54	38
Total	108	76
Total	242	148

The four interview questionnaires were highly structured with pre-coded categories offered to the respondents for their answers.   On the whole, the same questions were presented to both males and females, and since these were often more appropriate to the males, the interviews had a methodological sexist bias (as did the sampling decisions).

Given these constraints, it is possible to begin to offer a contribution to answering the questions set.   The data source is valuable in providing the opportunity to at least commence this task.

Position in the British economy

This group of young women school-leavers were entering the metropolitan labour markets of Birmingham and London for the first time over·the summer of 1971.   Unemployment was relatively high at the time although not in comparison with present levels and the figures stayed the same until late 1972 when the effects of the 'Barber boom' growth policies began to be felt.   This period of high demand lasted until 1974 but then unemployment began to increase again and continued to do so until the end of the period covered by this survey in 1976.   We can follow the labour market experiences of these young women through a cycle of trough to peak to trough fluctuations in the British economy.   It is against this cyclical background that the position of second generation West Indian young women's employment is now set.   ·The rare availability of a longitudinal data source provided a nearly unique opportunity to view, in a more dynamic sense, the interactions of these young women with the changes in the economic climate.

Both West Indian and white young women expressed a desire to obtain what can be described as 'women's jobs' on leaving school; these were clerical, sales and service workers (socio-economic group numbers 5 and 6) as Table 3.2 illustrates. In this sense all these young women had similar preferences, although the young black women could be said to be very slightly more ambitious than the whites. There was thus a matching of what are socialised preferences to the segregated opportunities for women's employment. However young black and white women, despite their similar educational starting point, did not have similar experiences as far as being successful in obtaining their desired jobs was concerned.

TABLE 3.2   *Job aspirations of women as recorded at the first interview**

Desired job using SEG classification	Percentages in each group**	
	West Indians	White
Intermediate non-manual (and above) 5	29	21
Junior non-manual, 6	60	66
Personal service, 7	3	8
Skilled manual, 9	3	2
Semi-skilled manual, 10	4	4
Unskilled manual, 11	–	–
Total	100	100

*   Individuals were asked what job they had wanted on leaving school. These jobs are coded using the OPCS socioeconomic group (SEG) classification.
** Figures are rounded to the nearest whole number.

It took black women longer than whites to secure their first jobs, even though the evidence suggested that they spent more time searching. Many school-leavers got jobs very quickly, while others had great difficulties resulting in lengthy periods of unemployment, and this was particularly so for the young black women. When the unemployment durations are stratified by level of education, for whites the amount of education was unimportant and having more qualifications did not necessarily shorten the process of securing a job. This was not the case with the black women where the reverse was true, and leaving school with some qualifications did help the transition from school to work to be effected more quickly.

At the end of their search black women were also less frequently successful in securing the job they had desired than whites were. Approximately 45 per cent of the black women obtained the job they had wanted at the end of their search or an acceptable substitute whereas 60 per cent of the whites had this experience. Thus during a time of low demand and a consequent shortage of more desirable jobs, young black women had more difficulties than whites in their employment experiences. Thus in terms of a labour queue, they appeared to be behind young white women, taking longer to secure jobs and being successful in obtaining their preferences less frequently. Having more education did appear to help West Indian women to secure jobs. We cannot prove discrimination with this sort of data, but given the matched nature of the samples, it does not seem unreasonable to suppose that employers, in this time of low demand were discriminating against black women school-leavers and giving preference to whites.

The jobs which they obtained after their transition from school to work can be seen in Table 3.3. The jobs were classified by the crude OPCS socio-economic-group (SEG) classifications, (8) but even so, the distributions illustrate

TABLE 3.3 *Socio-economic group of the jobs held by young women at the first interview*

Socio-economic group (OPCS classification)	Percentage in each group*	
	West Indian	White
1-6 Junior non-manual and above	78	87
7 Personal service	4	9
9 Skilled manual	4	1
10 Semi-skilled manual	14	4
11 Unskilled manual	1	—
Total	100	100
Number in sample**	104	115

* Percentages rounded to nearest whole number.

** Unemployed were excluded from the sample.

that one initial consequence of West Indian young women facing difficulties and being less successful than the whites was that they ended up with a higher proportion of less skilled jobs as a result. In drawing attention to this difference, the judgment is implied, of course, that semi-skilled work is less desirable than skilled and non-manual work although this may not be entirely appropriate when considering the broad categories of the OPCS classification. This issue of evaluating comparisons between black and white women's experiences is one which occurs as we go through these results. Where the judgment might be debatable I will state the viewpoint adopted here, but in this and some other cases, the fact that the young women's preferences expressed in this survey were for jobs other than those described as 'less skilled' is regarded as sufficient justification for the evaluation being made.

Unemployment is generally assumed to be less desirable than employment although, in the case of voluntary unemployment, any evaluation is not so unequivocal. The matter can sometimes be solved by a more detailed knowledge of the reasons behind, in this case, the unemployment experienced. The figures in Table 3.4 illustrate the varying experience of unemployment over the survey period of these two groups which broadly overlap with the national fluctuations described. The figures refer to unemployment when searching for work, and they do not have the problem of relying on individual's registration, which in the case of women, is a great handicap to be overcome in any attempt to assess the full extent of unemployment (Dex, 1978). The figures show that for this sample, women's unemployment fell as demand conditions improved prior to the third interview but rose again as the boom went into a decline before the fourth interview.

TABLE 3.4 *Unemployment frequencies at each interview** *(sample size in brackets)*

| Interview | London | | Birmingham | |
	West Indian	White	West Indian	White
1 (Feb. 1972)	9.0 (67)	8.0 (67)	18.5 (54)	5.6 (54)
2 (May 1973)	16.1 (56)	7.1 (56)	20.0 (50)	6.0 (50)
3 (Nov. 1974)	2.2 (45)	6.7 (45)	4.3 (46)	4.3 (46)
4 (Nov. 1976)	16.7 (36)	2.8 (36)	18.4 (38)	7.9 (38)

* 'Unemployed' here means 'not employed' and seeking work. When individuals were not employed and *not* seeking work they were excluded from the sample.

Several interesting features can be seen from the comparison between the young black and the white women. At times of high unemployment black women were often far more likely than whites to be unemployed whereas when demand improved (see Interview 3 results) their rates were either equal, or, in the case of London, better for black women. The frequency of unemployed West Indian young women, at most interviews, was usually higher in Birmingham than in London, although this discrepancy was not apparent between the white samples. London has traditionally been a slightly lower unemployment region than Birmingham so that the West Indian results are probably the more usual.

The extent to which the more frequent experience of unemployment was disadvantageous for these young black women can be partly assessed by comparing the record of their experiences of either a redundancy or a dismissal over the survey period. The figures which we have, which are likely to be an underestimate, (9) show that 35 per cent of the West Indians and 22 per cent of whites had at least one such involuntary experience during this five year period. This is a staggeringly high proportion and it is only tempered by the fact that the men's proportions were even higher. The reasons behind these figures are an obvious topic for further research. Thus the higher unemployment frequencies of young black women at each interview can be regarded as in part reflecting the greater difficulties they encountered in keeping jobs, as well as obtaining them. If there is a queue for hiring and for firing, West Indians seemed to be behind whites for hiring but in front for firing. We can conclude that West Indians fared worse than whites through the downswing in the economy, but benefited disproportionately in comparison with whites from an upswing.

The figures in Table 3.5 of the total durations of unemployment experienced over this survey show that at the end of the day, however, West Indian women were more disadvantaged in terms of their employment status than were similarly educated whites. Given that those in the sample who were 'lost' at earlier interviews were more likely to be those who had been unemployed at any earlier interview, the full extent of this differential is not reflected in these figures.

TABLE 3.5 *Total average duration of unemployment over the whole survey period (sample size in brackets)*

| | Mean duration in weeks | |
	London	Birmingham
West Indian	9.4	24.0
	(34)	(37)
White	4.2	11.1
	(34)	(37)

The last dimension of the position of this group of second generation West Indians in the British economy relates to the mean take-home-pay of the groups at the first and last interview. Pay was very similar between the two groups at the beginning and at the end of the period. Thus whilst West Indians did suffer in comparison with white young women in a number of ways mainly linked to their crossing the gateway into employment, their earnings opportunities at this stage appear to have been unaffected. The findings on take-home-pay may reflect different numbers of hours worked so that we cannot be sure that West Indians and whites have similar pay. Also, this result may be a consequence of the much narrower range of earnings open to women so that differentials are subdued (see Karen Stone's chapter in this volume).

The position of second generation West Indian women, in comparison with whites and as revealed by this sample, is one which can be seen to fluctuate as the economic climate fluctuated. The result that West Indian young women suffered disproportionately during a down-swing is one which is not particularly optimistic for the present high and rising unemployment rates, neither is it balanced out by the advantages during upswings. The most marked differentials between West Indians and whites were found in terms of recruitments and involuntary job separations culminating in longer unemployment durations for West Indian women.

These results provide a contribution to the attempt to answer the question about whether a permanent migrant's status exists. These second generation West Indian women were not so obviously in a segmented labour market sector in comparison with white women, at the beginning of their work experience, but in that they appeared to be behind whites for the advantages of either recruitment or job stability and in front for the disadvantages of involuntary separation, they constituted a more dispensable reserve army of labour, being kept to fill up the gaps. These are only tendencies, however, and by no means all West Indian young women were in these positions. There were differences between young black and white women employees which suggest that the young black women could have had worse prospects rather than lower status. In terms of the more conventional economic status measures of occupation and earnings, the narrower range of opportunities for women in employment appeared to dominate and produce a more uniform women's picture. But the fact that women can respond to these 'forces' means that the future is not wholly determined by these effects, however. Some of the responses which were enacted by this second generation West Indian sample will now be described in a way that tries to link together the economic position described above with aspects of the migration process as mediated by first generation migrant West Indian women.

Young black women's response

There are a number of characteristics emerging from the analysis of this sample of school-leavers which suggested that the young black women were reacting against the position of their mothers in the labour market.   The jobs of the total population of West Indian women, as recorded in the 1971 census are listed in Table 3.6 alongside the distribution of jobs held by the mothers of the West Indian young women in this sample.   The census figures reveal that large proportions of West Indian women were employed in semi-skilled manual jobs and in intermediate and junior non-manual, many of the non-manual being jobs in nursing.   By comparison with the census, the small sub-sample of West Indian mothers about whom information was available were in the same categories of jobs as the whole population, but to a greater extent in the semi- and unskilled manual jobs.   These mothers therefore had proportionately more lower status jobs than the whole West Indian women's population.

TABLE 3.6 *Socio-economic-group classification of the occupation of the mothers of these West Indian women as they left school, compared with the 1971 census distribution of West Indian women's occupations*

Socio-economic group Socio-economic group	Percentages in each group*	
	Occupation of mothers of West Indian women (where available)	1971 census** West Indian women
Professional and other non-manual, 1-4	—	1
Intermediate non-manual, 5	16	23
Junior non-manual, 6	5	13
Personal service, 7	8	10
Skilled manual, 9	8	8
Semi-skilled manual, 10	43	28
Unskilled, 11	19	17
Inadequately described		10
Total	100	100
Number in sample	37	

*   Percentages rounded to the nearest whole number.

**   *Source*:   1971 census.

As we saw earlier in Table 3.2, these West Indian school-leavers expressed particular preferences for non-manual jobs. In this way they were desiring a different set of jobs than those held by their mothers and West Indian women in general, and as such were reacting against their mother's position in the economic hierarchy.

The methods used by these young black women to secure their first (and subsequent) jobs on leaving school can be argued to illustrate a similar phenomenon; that is, a preference for jobs other than those held by their mothers. These young black women differed significantly from the whites in the way that they successfully obtained their jobs with young black women using the Youth Employment Service to a far greater extent than whites; the latter placed far more emphasis on the use of 'contacts'. This finding has been noted in other studies of second generation migrant school-leavers, of both young men and women (Dex, 1979a and Brooks and Singh, 1979). It suggests that these young black women were using formal channels in order to obtain a wider range of jobs than could be provided by their (mothers') 'contacts'. Even though the young black women were successful less frequently than whites, a comparison between the socio-economic group classification of mothers' occupations with daughters' first jobs (from Table 3.3 and Table 3.6) reveals that the second generation, at the outset did have a different set of jobs compared with their mothers, and with the West Indian women's labour force as a whole at the 1971 census. The younger women had very few semi- or unskilled manual jobs unlike the older women, but the young were in junior non-manual jobs to a greater extent than their elders and mothers. West Indian young women did have more semi-skilled jobs than the white school-leavers, however. How much of these differences is a product of age divisions between jobs in the women's labour market is impossible to tell from these data, but we must take seriously the idea that second generation West Indian women are determined to avoid filling the same position in British labour markets as their mothers.

Other positive responses, which have links with their mothers' values, were to be seen in these second generation women's enrolment on further education courses, in their attitudes towards women working and being trained, and in their marital status. Young black women took up and completed further education courses and examinations in much larger numbers than did the white females. This emphasis and value placed on education is one which has been found in other studies of West Indian women (Foner, 1979) and it may be a consequence of parental or mother's socialised transfer of preference to their offspring. It certainly is a feature which distinguished the young black from the young white women. In the case of whites, this lack of ambition for further

training and education was linked to a higher rate of marriage
by the end of this survey period, with 38 per cent of whites
compared to only 18 per cent of young black women having
married.   Young black women remained nominally 'single' to
a greater extent and these two behavioural characteristics, by
which West Indians and whites differed from each other, were
seen to have parallels in their attitudes towards the value of
education and training for women (ascertained at the third
interview).   Young black women gave positive responses to
questions which asked about the value of training for girls,
often to a much greater extent than did the young white
women.   Thus we see here more evidence for thinking that
West Indians placed great emphasis on education and training
for women both in their attitudes and in their behaviour.
Alongside this characteristic, the beginning of a different set
of family patterns from whites was found.

Karen Stone's chapter underlines and elaborates the conclusions of other studies (Foner, 1975; Phizacklea, 1982) which
indicates a much clearer set of employment-centred attitudes
amongst West Indian women than is found amongst mothers of
other ethnic groups.   But as Phizacklea (1982) comments this
is not some 'inherent' characteristic of West Indian women,
but a necessary response to a certain set of structural
features and related experience.

The suggestion that these second generation West Indian
young women chose to accept these positive links with their
parents' migration and background, but had more of a negative response to their mothers' status, occupation and contacts needs some further discussion.   The emphasis on education and training by these young West Indians, can be
viewed as making good sense in the context of their experiences in British labour markets which appear to use
education to position West Indian (if not white) women in a
labour recruitment queue.   As such, it is a rational and
positive response and it can be seen as an attempt to improve
or possibly maintain their position.   The fact that West
Indian young women's earnings were similar to those of whites
at the end of the survey may be due to extra qualifications
they had gained, although this would, if true, be further
evidence of discrimination since it only enabled them to keep
up with whites' earnings.   However the suggestion that it is
a positive response, and also having links with the migration
process remains.

This group of West Indian young women appeared to be responding to the labour market structures which they faced on
leaving school in ways which suggested that they had both
negative and positive reactions to their parents or mothers
and the migration process of which the first generation had
been a part.   Both responses can be described as revealing
responses in the second generation women which have strong
links both with the structural features of the sending society,

the migration process and the experiences of belonging to a racialised category in Britain. In that there is a response, West Indian young women were indicating their intention to resist filling a permanent migrant's position in the British economy drawing, where it seemed useful, on their West Indian roots and on the British economy's institutions.

CONCLUSIONS

The analysis undertaken here of a secondary data source of young black and white women school-leavers and their employment has been used to begin to offer answers to a number of questions about the place of young black women of West Indian parentage in the British economy. There are many ways in which it would be desirable to extend this analysis in order to answer the questions more fully. That position was seen to be one which changed in parallel with the fluctuations in the British economy and the young black women had to face a series of difficulties in obtaining and keeping jobs. They had, therefore, experiences of 'exclusion', presumably on grounds of colour, from British labour markets. Pressures were apparent which appeared to be working in the direction of making young black women into a reserve army labour force. It is clear, however, from this investigation that the suggestion that being black in labour markets is not as significant as the overriding importance of being a woman is at best a half truth. The overall position of these West Indian women was worse than that of their matched white school-mates. This could be argued to be a permanent migrants' status but it is not the whole story.

A large group of these West Indian young women, although only a minority, responded to these forces of exclusion and began to generate 'inclusive' responses. These have strong links with the role model provided by their mothers, with the migration process experienced by their mothers and with the fact that the majority of West Indian women participate in the paid employment sector in Britain. The form of the links, for the second generation, whether positive or negative, was decided by the nature of their interactions and experiences in British labour markets over this five year period.

In that we were able to compare young black with young white women both of whom could be thought to be a 'second generation' women's labour force, some interesting findings emerged. Using the indicators available young black women in this sample did appear to be more employment-orientated and less home-orientated than the whites, a result which is probably linked as mentioned to the first generation migrants' status of their West Indian mothers. This experience meant that large proportions of their mothers came to Britain seeking economic opportunities, often being prepared to become independent, or alter their domestic relationships for that reason, and in this way differentiating themselves from white indigenous women (at least in a statistical sense).

The extra difficulties faced by young black women during the times of rising unemployment mean that the present trend of high and rising unemployment promises a bleaker future to these women. Their positive responses however, learnt through the migration process of their parents and in facing, for themselves, discrimination in British labour markets, may provide them with a useful resource with which to be active in facing the future. It will also be interesting to see the emergence of new sets of kinship relationships between mothers and daughters to replace those which were broken during migration. The fact that West Indian second generation women and their unemployment is not 'news' in the same way that it is for men should not prevent our identifying their problems. Nor should we fail to recognise the ways in which they are responding in the face of very severe difficulties, despite this almost complete lack of concern.

NOTES

1 I wish to acknowledge the Department of Employment for allowing me to use the data source which is described in this paper and their funding of another analysis of the same source, without which the work contained in this paper would not have been possible. The views expressed and the responsibility for errors are mine.

2 See for example groups of articles in 'New Community' under the headings Youth and the Second Generation, vol. VI, no. 3, 1978, Minority children and Young People, vol. VII, no. 2, 1979 and The Younger Generation, vol. VII, no. 3, 1979. These are only a selection of the most recent work. See also Commission for Racial Equality (1978).

3 See Tomlinson (1978), and Rampton Report (1981) for the evidence of underachievement. Driver (1980) has questioned whether underachievement characterises West Indian young women in particular but the latest evaluation of the evidence by the Rampton Committee suggests underachievement is widespread.

4 The role of women in the economy constitutes very much an ongoing debate, see Barrett (1980) and West (1982) for summaries of these debates. For instance, women have been viewed as welfare supports to the male breadwinner in a way that either is sexually subordinating and dependent (see e.g. Barker and Allen, 1976, 1976a) or that is helping more positively to boost male wages by staying at home (e.g. Humphries, 1977).

5 The totals derived from these samples had a far greater number in London than in Birmingham which led the OPCS

to decide to supplement the Birmingham sample by finding West Indians who qualified and who left school in 1972. This decision caused more disadvantageous complications than the extra numbers were beneficial.

6　Those 'lost' from the sample at the second, third and fourth interviews were disproportionately those who had been unemployed at their earlier interviews. This was particularly the case for the West Indians and it means that unemployment experiences for the group as a whole were underrecorded.

7　Information about the experiences of unemployment were collected in full, however, but job changes were under-recorded. Individuals who indicated that they had permanently withdrawn from the labour market at any inter-view were then dropped from the sample. 'Permanent' here is restricted in its meaning. It means that they indicated that they were not seeking work at the time and did not intend to, over the rest of the planned survey period. This decision obviously excluded many more females than males and therefore had quite serious conse-quences for the female sample. It illustrates a certain shortsightedness of sexist thinking that only the formal paid employment sector is of interest.

8　For example, both skilled and unskilled non-manual female clerical and shop assistants' jobs are both classified as SEG No. 6 'junior non-manual'.

9　Individuals were asked at the later interviews whether they had changed their jobs between interviews and if they had why they had left their previous job. If they had changed jobs more than once between interviews, the job separation reasons were not recorded for more than the most recent change.

4 Sexual divisions and ethnic adaptation: the case of Greek-Cypriot women

Floya Anthias

Greek-Cypriots, the largest linguistic minority in London, enjoy in common with other New Commonwealth migrants who arrived prior to 1971 the same political-legal rights as the indigenous population. However, unlike black migrants from the New Commonwealth they do not suffer racialisation as such. Historically, racism was constructed through the medium of slave society and not only colonialism. But racism is dynamically constituted and can be attached to any difference that has an 'ethnic' character - that is, posits an essential culture or locus of 'origin'. What was foreign-white-exotic yesteryear may become racial and undesirable this year.

Economically, the position of Greek-Cypriot men is rather different from other New Commonwealth migrants in that rather than acting as replacement labour for jobs vacated by the indigenous population they have tended to fill vacancies left by earlier minorities, like Jews in clothing and Italians in the catering industry, many moving into a petty-bourgeois class position. Cypriot women on the other hand (like other migrant women) have taken over the jobs that indigenous women had abandoned for the more stable and desirable white-collar service sectors. Cypriots as a whole have formed an ethnic economy that contains certain elements of an informal economy.

As colonial migrants Greek-Cypriots bring with them cultural visibility, low language and occupational skills, low educational qualifications and non-initiation into the structural 'openings' and cultural expectations of British society. Ethnic disadvantage in Britain is not only linked to racism or the cultural characteristics of migrant groups, however, but is implicated in structures of employment, housing and access to the state. These structures are 'managed' or 'negotiated' by ethnic groups in different ways through ethnic and class action. Migrant groups draw upon ethnic and class resources which are dynamically re-constructed in the new setting of advanced capitalism and the 'opportunities' it provides for the incorporation of migrant 'skills' and 'preferences'.

This chapter is concerned with the way in which ethnicity and sexual divisions are used by Greek-Cypriot men for the 'management' of ethnic or migrant disadvantage and for the achievement of the economistic aims of migration: (1) Cypriot women we argue suffer a 'triple burden' as women, as migrants and as workers for migrant men. This is not unique to

Cypriot women but is the case for all those migrant groups
whose adaptation has taken the form of small-scale entrepreneurial activity in the backwaters of capitalist production.
This activity is usually in labour-intensive concerns that are
increasingly shifting to the Third World itself where labour,
and in particular female migrant labour from the rural areas,
is cheap and freely available.   Greek-Cypriot women are a
source of cheap migrant labour and their employment often
involves the extension of the patriarchal relations of the
family to those of work.   This does not mean that Greek-
Cypriot men themselves do not suffer migrant disadvantage,
but only that it is women who have borne the brunt of the
migrant adaptation of a fairly significant proportion of men
who have used their ethnicity successfully in British society.
But even here, such men have experienced a cultural and
personal impoverishment through being involved in a spiral of
money-making that is only possible with the total sacrifice of
leisure and time to the demands of a highly unstable business
sector - the small concerns of the clothing and service sectors.   Cypriot male employees are also exploited by ethnic employers, but there is a sexual division of labour as we shall
see and greater opportunities for them to move into small-
scale business themselves with capital accumulation made
through working long hours and doing shift work.

Greek-Cypriot men and women are 'migrant labour' alongside other New Commonwealth migrants.   They formed part
of the wave of New Commonwealth migration during the 'long
boom' period of the British economy in the 1950s and 1960s.
All Commonwealth immigration is characterised by being economically motivated and was drawn to those areas where the
demand for unskilled labour was highest.   The debate on
'cultural choice or ethnic disadvantage' has tended to take a
polarised position in explaining the jobs and the housing of
migrants.   For us cultural choices are made within the framework of ethnic disadvantage.   In this way ethnic segregation
may help in the management of the latter both in terms of
work and in terms of housing.

The Cypriot population is a fairly concentrated and visible
one in London.   Haringey and Islington in North London are
the two boroughs with the largest number of Cypriots.   It
has been estimated that the Cypriot population is in the
region of 160,000 to 170,000, (2) three-quarters of which are
Greek-Cypriot and the remainder Turkish-Cypriot.   The vast
majority of these, about three-quarters, live in Greater
London.   The Cypriot population in England is fairly young,
only 8 per cent of men and 7 per cent of women were forty-
five years or over in 1971 (Commission for Racial Equality,
1979).

According to the 1971 census, (3) Greek-Cypriot employment
patterns differ considerably from other New Commonwealth
groups (which themselves present different characteristics).

The main difference is the marked degree to which Cypriot males are self-employed; 22.9 per cent as compared with 7 per cent for the New Commonwealth total, and relative to other New Commonwealth groups the large proportion who are employers and managers. Over half of self-employed Cypriot males have employees. However Cypriot men have a lower representation in the 'professional employees' category than the New Commonwealth as a whole.

A second characteristic of Cypriot male employment is the high proportion who are service workers (22.6 per cent) compared to 6.5 per cent for the New Commonwealth total and 6.2 per cent for men from Pakistan, 2.8 per cent for men from India and 3.5 per cent for men from the West Indies. In addition 12 per cent of Cypriot men are engineering workers and 7 per cent are labourers. These constitute the largest categories.

Cypriot women show a lower economic activity rate (43.5 per cent) than New Commonwealth women overall (49.8 per cent). Nevertheless, our own research indicates that much female labour is unregistered and we shall consider the factors for this later. Cypriot female labour overall is more concentrated in the pre-industrial clothing and service sectors of the economy and under-represented in the professional and other non-manual categories. If we consider the social class position of Cypriot women and New Commonwealth women we find that Cypriot women are more clustered in the manual categories of skilled (16.9 per cent) and semi-skilled (32.5 per cent) than New Commonwealth women overall (8.8 per cent and 29 per cent) and are less represented in both professional (0.3 per cent compared to 1.5 per cent) and intermediate categories (7.5 per cent compared to 21.2 per cent). In this sense we would argue that despite the prevalence of racist ideology in British society 'Cypriot' women have a more subordinate position in the labour market than other New Commonwealth women. However, all female migrant labour shares certain characteristics of female labour as a whole which is clustered within particular sectors of the labour market (see Phizacklea in the Introduction), such as the clothing, clerical and service sectors. Thus although certain of the political and ideological conditions it enjoys are those of migrant labour the conditions for the sale of that labour are those of sexual divisions - domestic labour, child care and the bourgeois family.

This chapter will analyse the way in which Greek-Cypriot women's labour is used as the cornerstone of the Greek-Cypriot ethnic economy in Britain. We shall also consider the extent to which migration and economic participation has had a progressive and liberating effect on Greek-Cypriot women. Before so doing however it is necessary to provide a short discussion of the traditional Greek-Cypriot family and the position of rural women in Cyprus around the time of

emigration.   A continuing 'home orientation' and an 'ideology
of return' exists for Greek-Cypriot migrants which makes this
discussion even more pertinent.   It is within this context
that the position of Greek-Cypriot women in Britain has to be
seen.

WOMEN IN CYPRUS AND THE TRADITIONAL GREEK-CYPRIOT FAMILY

The traditional Cypriot family is rooted in a primarily agricultural economy characterised by peasant small-holdings.   Some
light manufacturing and industrial production had developed
by the 1950s in Cyprus but it was mainly organised in small
units.   Cyprus is a classic case of a small island with no
economic interest for colonialism that has suffered almost con-
tinual colonisation.   After a series of colonial masters which
in recent times has included both the Ottomans (from 1571-
1878) and Britain (1878-1960) it achieved 'independence' in
1960.   The economic conditions in Cyprus until independence
were structured by colonial policy which failed to encourage
local industrial production and provided favourable conditions
.for the importation and sale of British goods.
   The population of Cyprus is primarily Greek-Cypriot (80
per cent).   In addition a Turkish-Cypriot Moslem population
constituting up to 1974 18 per cent of the population has existed since 1571, but we shall confine ourselves to examining
the family within the Greek-Orthodox population.
   The Greek-Cypriot family can be seen as a variant of a
particular Mediterranean family type which itself presents a
heterogeneity of nuclear and extended family forms.   What
has been seen to characterise it however has been the social
importance of female sexual purity.   It is nuclear in ideal
form but may at times include cohabitation by other members
of the family, especially widowed parents.   Kinship is bilateral and marriage is forbidden to the fifth degree, i.e.
second cousins may not marry.   Property is transmitted bi-
laterally amongst offspring and this accounts for the great
degree of land fragmentation in Cyprus.   An arranged marriage system exists whereby the parents are centrally involved
in a 'collective decision' (Saint-Cassia 1981) which includes the
right of veto by the prospective bride and groom.   In this
arrangement discussions concerning the transfer of property
to the daughter through the dowry form are made, which for
the last forty years or so at least has generally meant the
provision by the girl's parents of a house on marriage.
Girls with no house find it difficult to marry through 'normal'
channels and competition is often debilitating for prospective
bridegrooms who are able to make exhorbitant demands.
   Girls are expected to be sexually innocent at marriage and
contact between the sexes is limited.   In the towns and

amongst the more educated, social gatherings and outings of single men and women are permitted. However, men are not expected to be sexually pure and there is an encouragement to find sexual outlets to prove their 'manhood'. This usually means a resort to prostitutes or to the few girls who have a 'low' reputation and are regarded as 'outcasts' or to foreign girls who come as tourists or to work. Women until fairly recently could be divorced on discovery that they were not virgins on their marriage night and the old and now largely defunct custom of publicly displaying the bloodied bedsheet is rooted in this.

Marriage in Cyprus means for men and women the attainment of full adult status. For women, failure to marry involves a total abnegation of sexuality and the continuing dominance of the father. There are no alternative life-styles in Cyprus, making it difficult for women to struggle against patriarchal modes of control. Social marginalisation is the inevitable result of failure to marry.

The concept of honour (filotimo) is applied to women as 'timi' as the possession of honour. For the man on the other hand, it is the orientation or love of honour that is important. For women 'timi' denotes sexual innocence, obedience and domesticity. As Juliet du Boulay (1974) notes, the conception of female sexuality involves the possibility of 'impurity'. Women are the potential victims to their own sexuality which they must be protected from and they are seen as essentially carnal. A woman's loss of honour reflects on the males who control her for they are finally responsible. Men must therefore strive to keep their honour through the control of their family and 'their' women.

The public performance of conformity to the norm of male dominance is supreme, the wife showing respect and submission although no public expression of affection is made except by engaged couples. Although the norm of public submissiveness to the male is dominant certain deviations are allowed especially where a woman has been forced to marry a man who is 'beneath' her or where she is totally economically independent from him. There is a recognition therefore that masculine 'honour' is related to his role as chief 'provider' and there is a certain fear of a woman who 'earns' more than her husband.

Women in Cyprus are totally responsible for the domestic domain and children, even where they work for wages. The relation between 'honour' and 'masculinity' asserts that it is demeaning for men to do the 'feminine' tasks of child care, cleaning and washing and if they do they are not exercising proper control of the female. The majority of men believe that they should help in the home only when their wife is too ill or the work too heavy. Women's domestic role extends to services in agriculture and where the male has other paid work, is regarded as her sole responsibility. Most women

are at their husband's or father's beck and call, often being
made to leave the table countless times to bring some extra
food or drink - the best food is reserved for the men and
women generally leave themselves last to be served.
Women in Cyprus have always been involved in production
for in the traditional peasant agriculture-based economy,
women and to a lesser extent, children's labour was essential
to the subsistence of the family unit.   They not only worked
alongside their husbands in the fields, but as Surridge (1930,
p. 26) notes 'if the holding is insufficient to maintain the
family, to work as agricultural labourers on the roads'.   In
addition women weaved cloth on primitive looms and in certain
areas, such as Larnaca, Limassol and Nicosia they made lace
which they sold, many through selling outlets in Lefkara.
Children too were involved in production often working for
other people, long hours from 'sunrise to half an hour before
sunset' with a two-hour break.   Many girls in addition
worked as domestic servants or 'Kores' (literally virgins).
Many of these were employed as young as eight years of age
and most worked long hours, doing heavy work.   Some employers provided dowries but many girls were ill-treated and
sexually assaulted at times.
In addition to work in the fields women were responsible for
tending the animals, collecting the yield from carob and olive
trees, producing olive oil, fetching water from the well or
village fountain, making halloumi (a cheese made from goats'
or sheep's milk), grinding corn and wheat into flour and
pourgouri (cracked wheat), making 'trahanas' (soup from
wheat and yogurt) and drying it, making the family's clothes,
as well as cooking, cleaning, tending the children and all the
other tasks of 'domestic labour'.   Much of this employment
was hidden in the household for it did not reap a wage and
merged into domestic production yielding use values.   Halloumi, cloth, trahanas, olive oil and other produce may also have
been for exchange.
These conditions still existed up to the 1950s although
urbanisation and the growth of light manufacturing and the
construction industry were on the ascent.
Young single women came over from the villages of Cyprus
in the 1950s and early 1960s on their own to stay with relatives and to work for their dowries.   Rural underemployment
and chronic indebtedness were features of Cypriot peasant life
during this period and many parents were unable to provide
for their daughters.   Also there was a demographic imbalance
in Cyprus which accounts for many girls seeking to come over
to England to find a husband.   However most women came
over as young married women following their husband one or
two years after he had migrated.   Single women from poorer
families came over to foster their life-chances which were minimal in the Cyprus context and they must be seen as migrant
labour and as fulfilling their goal of marriage - which is an

important economic as well as personal and social relation.
Married women came over to join their husbands but from the
beginning found it necessary to take work in order to fulfil
the economistic aim of migration.

GREEK-CYPRIOT WOMEN IN LONDON

Greek-Cypriots emigrate for primarily economic reasons and to
provide better opportunities for their children.   Given the
economic aspirations and the desire to accumulate a nest-egg
for eventual return to Cyprus, it became a necessity for
women to work too.   It was however unthinkable for women
brought up in the enclosed world of traditional Cypriot rural
life (the majority of migrants being rural inhabitants) to enter
into unskilled manual work in foreign and 'dangerous' male-
regulated territory.   There was the additional factor of language and lack of self-confidence since most women had only
worked at home or in the fields, for the Cyprus economy was
agriculturally based until the 1960s by which time most emigration had been completed.   Women were afraid of independent thought and action and men too felt it a threat to their
'honour' to send their women to work in such conditions.
When men sent over for their wives and families they had
often worked in Britain for a year or more, as waiters, shoe-
makers or tailors and some had accumulated a small amount of
capital.   Their aspirations were to have their own small
family business, which was related to their earlier role as
peasant producers but also linked to exclusions from other
openings because of lack of language skills and educational
qualifications.   In addition rents for cafes and small restaurants were cheap in the central areas of north London that
they moved into.   The earlier establishment of a caucus of
Greek-Cypriot migrants was a relevant factor in the eventual
geographical settlement of Greek-Cypriots.   Small Greek-
Cypriot owned cafes would employ their womenfolk and were
only viable given their employment.   The earliest clothing
factories were small family concerns - often two or three
brothers or relations setting up a small business on limited
capital, filling the openings left by the declining clothing
manufacturing sector (the East- and West-End 'sweat shops').
The boom period of the British economy in the 1950s and
1960s had increased worker expectations and aspirations and
the conditions, pay and instability of this sector of the labour
market left openings for migrant labour.   In addition women
brought the traditional sewing and cooking skills with them
which could be exploited in this setting.   From its inception,
Cypriot female migrant labour provided a pool of often unpaid
or at least cheap labour involving the direct extension of production for use into production for exchange and of the patriarchal relations of the family into wage-labour.

The 'typical' Greek-Cypriot woman in England works either
in a clothing firm as a machinist or finisher, as a homeworker, or works alongside and for her husband in the many
restaurants, cafes and shops that characterise Greek-Cypriot
centres of residence like Haringey in London.   There is a
tendency however amongst younger women to work in clerical
and secretarial work and in hairdressing.   Greek-Cypriot
women often work for Greek-Cypriot employers and we argue
were the building block of Greek-Cypriot entrepreneurship.

We shall now examine more carefully the links between
sexual divisions at work and the nature of Greek-Cypriot
ethnic and economic adaptation by looking at the Cypriot
clothing industry.

As already noted Greek-Cypriot women went into the
clothing sector and so did men on the presumption of the
skills of women who traditionally made clothes.   The entry of
Cypriots into this sector is therefore already premised on (a)
the skills of women, and (b) the needs of women to work in
the 'migrant' situation, and (c) the overriding economic motivation for migration.   The earliest employment of women was
either in catering with their husbands or in the clothing industry.   In the latter case women took out-work since it
was difficult either to find day-time child care or get help
with children after school.   This also suited the employer
who thus had a labour-force totally under the control of the
demand for labour.   Those who chose to work in factories
tended to be on piece-rates which gave them flexibility, and
employers benefited from not having to pay a fixed wage.
When women worked in factories where pay was better and
employment more regular, their children were often left with
unqualified child-minders (many themselves migrants) who may
have cared for five or more small children.

One of the features of the clothing industry is that it is
characterised by small-scale factories dependent for production on large-scale companies.   The Cypriot clothing firms
are not strictly speaking manufacturers but 'outdoor units' or
contractors.   As the large manufacturers supply them with
orders, this entails two problems.   Firstly the supply
depends on each firm being able to compete successfully for
the large manufacturers.   Secondly, supply is subject to
fluctuations in the market for women's clothing (which is very
unstable).   Thus, entering the clothing industry always requires the willingness to take on large risks and many small
firms close every year, especially during periods of economic
recession.

The almost total dependence on orders from large-scale firms
and the possibility of these being withdrawn have two effects:
1 One is that small Greek-Cypriot firms, often working with
   the minimum of full-time employees and relying on a diver-
   gent home-working force, attempt to make it work as hard
   and efficiently as possible to meet rigid submission dates
   for production.

2 A second is that there is a tendency not to register all
full-time workers so that the employer avoids redundancy
payments when he lays off these staff - a common occur-
rence given the unpredictability of the supply of orders
from the large manufacturers. The Greek-Cypriot factory
employer is himself in a master/servant relation to the
larger employer and is the medium by which his fellow-
countrymen are exploited, often to ensure his own survival.
The workforce within the clothing industry is primarily
female. Many firms in Haringey are located in larger buildings vacated by larger firms who have left London and some
are located in previously residential buildings - that is they
are implicated in the urban and industrial decay syndrome
mentioned by many ·writers and a crucial element in Phizacklea's and Miles's (1980) study of Willesden. The cost of
renting these premises tends to be low and the firms rely on
employing as small a permanent workforce as possible, depending often on homeworkers who can be easily disposed of, for
much of their work.
Women who are the mainstay of the Cypriot clothing industry are susceptible to high unemployment, low job security
and little protection.
Within the clothing industry there is a sexual division of
labour in two senses. Firstly, women tend to be employees
whereas men are more likely to be employers. Secondly,
women are usually machinists, finishers or overlockers whereas men are pressers and cutters. Men, on the whole, earn
much more than women, the difference being often as much as
100 per cent with overtime. Men however also face problems
of the instability of the industry and often suffer similar
results ensuing from the non-registration of the workforce.
Men and women are often segregated and women are very con-
scious of the sexual implications of male work-contacts preferring to work with relatives, co-villagers or acquaintances -
'gnostous' where possible. Piece-rate is a common practice
for machinists and this again provides the employer with the
advantage of not having to pay a guaranteed wage especially
at times of low output. Women are usually unaware of the
way in which employers are able to escape their statutory
obligations. For example, women are usually paid a net-wage
without a proper payslip. The employer may or may not
register her and may or may not pay national insurance contributions which she needs to be properly covered for sickness, unemployment and retirement benefit. A common practice is to declare a low wage and/or low hours of work.
Thus women who work - usually 36-40 hours a week or more -
may be registered only as part-time workers with all that
implies. For example, Maria worked for different Cypriot employers full-time as a finisher from 1957 to 1972 - most days
working from 9 am to 7 pm and receiving extra payment
between 5-7 pm. This was worked out on the basis of her

full-time pay and not at a higher overtime rate. She
believed that her national insurance contributions were being
paid but when she retired in 1972 discovered she was only
eligible for a small proportion of the state pension. Employers also often fail to regard safety regulations. For
example Ellou fell down some concrete steps in her factory
and broke her leg. She was thus out of employment for
three months and then it took some time for her fully to re-
cover. The employer had failed to provide adequate lighting
and thus was responsible. He however denied responsibility,
failed to compensate her and indeed sacked her on the
grounds that he could not keep her job open until she recov-
ered. It was suggested to Ellou that she should take him to
court but she was unwilling as she did not want to create
trouble for a fellow 'Cypriot' and 'all the community would
find out'. This would lead to her stigmatisation as a dis-
loyal employee and 'Cypriot'.

Women often place more emphasis on the exact amount of *net*
pay they receive than on the conditions of employment, the
granting of holiday with pay and the conformity of employers
to statutory obligations which are in the interests of their
labour force. Indeed, women who are on a weekly wage, are
often not allowed time off with pay for sickness, child care or
other reasons. What is common is that pay is deducted at an
hourly rate for all absence from work, including lateness.
The lunch break is often only half an hour and if the women
are on piece-rate, many work through it. Women are often
laid off before their holiday time is due and employers often
close up for 4-5 weeks in the summer months to go back to
Cyprus and do not compensate their work-force.

The following are examples which illustrate the position of
Cypriot women in the clothing industry in 1981.

Androulla is a 36-year-old clothing machinist who came over
to work for her uncle and then was a homeworker for the
first cousin of her brother's wife. Her husband has to
know the environment she works at and doesn't like her to
move around. She is now in her third factory since 1961.
In her last factory her previous employer told his workforce they didn't make the value of their wages. She was
receiving £70 clear for a five-day week from 8.30-6 pm.
Her employer kept on insisting she work harder. Pressers
(men) in that particular factory earned over £100 and
cutters over £120 per week but could make much more on
overtime. Some got over £140 per week. Older women
tended to be finishers and earned less - £50-£60 was the
range.

The husband didn't 'mind' her working but preferred her
not to but they couldn't survive without it. She is tired
of work, tired of noise and tired of her life here so wants
to return to Cyprus.

Thekla is a finisher in a small factory.   She earns £55 per
5-day week, from 8.30-6 pm with 3/4 hour break at lunch
and a 1/4 hour for tea.   If she is one minute over, her employer complains.   She has worked for eight different
firms in the last 15 years.   In the previous one her employer borrowed £100 from her and did a 'bunk'.   She
knows that other women at work, doing the same job, earn
a little more.   But she has problems with her eyes - she
is blind in one.   This employer is quite good - he is
young and only started two years ago.   She worked for an
employer previously for six years and he sacked her
because she 'wasn't quick enough'.   Thekla is often under
duress to finish the order and she is often shouted at.
She comes home in tears some days.   At Christmas and
other holidays she is not always paid for holiday-time.
Her boss gives her a small present instead.

Christine is 40 years old.   She works for her cousin.
She is a highly skilled machinist and takes home £80 a week
(with overtime).   She has worked for the same firm (it is
a large one with over sixty people) for five years.   Her
cousin has helped her daughters 'settle', found them husbands and provided financial help.   She is very pleased
but some of the other women complain.
Often a woman is selected as an ally by the employer and as
a spy on the workforce.   Such women mediate between the
two and can manipulate in their own interests.
Husbands are often suspicious of their wives if they come
back late from the factory.   Yiota (32) has a husband who
regularly beats her up if she is late.   He calls her a
'whore'.   But she wants to stay with him.   She has a
small child and could not cope on her own.

Froso has an employer who 'raped' her at the factory but
she is too frightened to tell because her husband will leave
her.   She has to subject herself to him as she is frightened he might tell her husband.
The range of pay is between £70 and £80 per week for
machinists for a 40-hour week and between £50 and £60 for
finishers.   Many women have had to take a wage-cut with the
recent economic crisis, and firms tend to pass on their own
problems to their workers.   For example the Inland Revenue
has launched a campaign against payment of 'clear wages' and
tax evasion and some firms are going 'bankrupt' in order to
avoid investigation.   Others are giving lower 'clear wages' to
women in order to meet the statutory requirements and not
take a cut in profits.   Most women have no choice but to
accept although there are some signs of a growing 'class'
consciousness.   Most Cypriot dress factories are small and
enclosed communities, people establishing personal bonds, and
the employer-employee relationship is underpinned by ethnic

and familial networks. This makes infiltration by the
organised unions very difficult. In any case the networks
within the Greek-Cypriot community are such that once a
worker becomes identified as a 'disruptive' or 'unionised' element he/she finds it difficult to get work within the 'ethnic
economy'. This is true despite the affiliation of many employers and workers to AKEL, the Communist Party of Cyprus
and its branch in London (formed in 1974).

Although Greek-Cypriot firms are often themselves, as
noted, in a master/servant relation to the manufacturer and
have little capital to fall back on at times of crisis, their
manipulation of the labour force involves an assertion of shared
'class' interests which is possible on the basis of 'ethnic'
loyalty and honour. For Cypriot employers and workers
often attend the same weddings, may have known each other
in Cyprus, often establish 'fictive' kin links where there are
no 'natural' ones, and are seen as sharing similar opportunities and disadvantages in British society. In any case the
aspirations of the male workforce are to be themselves self-
employed, and many men often make a transition from 'wage-
labourer' to 'small capitalist' within a few years. Profits by
small firms are often undeclared so that tax is evaded and
Greek-Cypriot accountants are employed who 'cook' the books.
The use of 'cabbage' (left-over material from the order, made
into clothing) provides a retail supply of clothing to the
Greek-Cypriot community at much lower cost than in normal
retail outlets.

Unionisation has not penetrated into the Cypriot clothing
industry. There are various reasons for this often involving
the use of the 'ethnic' category to obfuscate the class category. Even amongst left organisations this problem is
underplayed and ethnic interests within the community are
seen as more important than any class differentiations. This
is partly linked to the common class background of immigrants,
self-employed or wage-labour. Most came from the urban and
rural displaced population, all finding similar exclusions in
British society vis-à-vis language, skills and culture. All
share the 'cultural stuff' of the importance of 'honour', 'the
family' and 'the sexual purity' of women. All have shared
their experience of British ethnicity via British colonialism.
They all see themselves as potential employers and as noted
already there is much movement amongst the males in this
direction. As regards women we can single out five factors
contributing to their unwillingness to organise in the workplace:

1 Women do not usually conceptualise the employer as an ex-
  ploiter for through the dominance of the ethnic category
  there occurs identification with him. Kin ties and village
  and social network ties make a class conceptualisation and
  any ensuing militancy quite 'impracticable'.
2 Women themselves are reluctant to 'organise' in unions

because they perceive themselves to have separate interests (from other women) and particular (in relation to men) needs within the Cypriot context. Fear of stigmatisation and disloyalty to the 'friends' - the employer/employee relation is often expressed in this idiom - is a major factor here. Women often ask for higher wages and complain as individuals but to organise a movement or within a movement for this purpose is unacceptable to them.

3 Women often 'know' that to jeopardise their job is not worthwhile since opportunities for them outside the clothing industry are limited and they prefer the work context of the 'Cypriot' firm. They often do not know to what extent they are disadvantaged in their conditions of employment, since they do not mix freely with other sections of the population.

4 Women often feel they get a 'good deal' and often 'boast' of the sums they can make as piece-workers especially. Some may take a net pay of £80-£100 per week. The pay of women in Cyprus is very low (less than £20 per week on average) so Greek-Cypriot women in London regard their own wages as quite astonishing despite being made up by working long hours under poor conditions.

5 There is no effort within the Greek-Cypriot community to organise women at work. The left and linked organisations may fear losing support if they did so and their members have their own stake as employers. There is also a belief that other openings in the labour market are worse and that it is in the overall interests of the Greek-Cypriot community not to 'interfere' - these interests are defined as those of its males who are the chief 'bread-winners'.

In Haringey, only two firms have individual members belonging to the NUTGW (National Union of Tailoring and Garment Workers). Nationally this organises 40 per cent of workers in the clothing industry, 90 per cent of members being women - it appears that the nature of small firms hinders organisation for it is the larger firms that tend to be unionised.

The only Cypriot organisation formed to represent economic interests within the Cypriot community is DACA, the employers' union (Dressmakers' and Allied Contractors' Association). This has a membership of about eighty firms, mainly Greek-Cypriot, and aims to compete with manufacturers by going straight to the retailers. Thus it is an organisation aimed to destroy the dependence of small firms on the large manufacturing companies and expresses class interests vis-à-vis them. The location of the 'class enemy' has been possible in this instance, where it has not been possible for the workforce, because of the interference for the latter of the 'ethnic' category in the formation of 'class' consciousness.

Of fundamental importance is that DACA has created a situation whereby employers:

are now in a position to agree on wage rates and keep wages

down as much as possible, therefore increasing employers'
profit margins (Haringey Employment Project, 1980, p. 18).
DACA has also been able, along with Cypriot clothing employers as a whole, to promote the practice of relocating the
assembly stage of production to Cyprus where labour is much
cheaper, resulting in less work for machinists in Britain.
In addition despite the resistance of NUTGW they have been
able to secure funds for a training scheme from local
councils.

Homeworkers

We have already noted that much female employment in the
clothing industry is non-enumerated for various reasons.
One particular section who failed to appear, more or less, in
any official statistics are homeworkers.

National conditions and surveys of homeworkers are relevant
to a consideration of the particular position of Greek-Cypriot
women.   The estimates of the extent of homeworking vary
from 13,000 to approximately 150,000 (Crine, 1979).   Surveys have consistently shown the poor working conditions and
pay of such women and the problems involved in their ambig-
uous employment status.   The TUC definition of homework
is:

work done in the home for another person, or for sale to
another person.

The majority of homeworkers are not protected by trades
union membership; their isolation, insecurity and the small
firms involved make this particularly difficult.   If they ask
for more wages as individuals they may lose their job.   They
lack employee status, are often defined by their employer as
'self-employed' and thus lack the rights of employees to an
itemised pay-slip, specified terms and conditions of employment, holiday and maternity leave, redundancy pay or appeal
against 'unfair dismissal'.

The distinct advantages to the employer are obvious. Firstly he is not entering a contract with specified obligations and
can therefore provide work when and how he chooses and can
dismiss the homeworker - if necessary without fearing any
ramifications and without compensation.   Secondly he is not
paying for heating, machinery, lighting or rent - i.e. has no
overheads.   Thirdly since she is isolated and vulnerable, he
can pay her lower rates of pay than a 'normal' employee - she
often has little choice but to accept.   The majority of women
are tied to the home because of child-care requirements and/or
domestic responsibilities or through some form of disability or
having to care for disabled relatives.

This is particularly the case for Greek-Cyrpiot women who
may not be aware of whatever limited child-care provisions
exist and/or are less willing to search aggressively for them.

Their general lack of skills also makes the choice of part-time work, offering flexible hours, almost non-existent.   Cypriot women work for economic reasons - not out of choice.

In a recent local homeworking campaign in Haringey, various Greek-Cypriot organisations were represented including the Greek-Cypriot Women's Organisation (Union of Cypriot Women).   What was striking, however, was the absence of homeworkers themselves from the meetings that were open to the public and had been extensively publicised by the Greek-Cypriot press in London ('Parikiaki Haravgi' and 'Vema'). This was due to the 'deep-rooted suspicions' that homeworkers have of the council.   This suspicion gives much credence to our view that the extent of female employment is much larger than the official data registers.   The confirmation that home-workers do not register their employment is found also in the study by Hope et al. (1976).

There are various reasons offered by Greek-Cypriot women for homeworking.   One is that it allows them to maintain their domestic responsibilities to the satisfaction of an often highly demanding husband and children.   Many women say that they like to devote time to tending to their housework, cooking and shopping.   Another reason, an important one we believe, is that many homeworkers. if not most, have dependent children of a pre-school age and either prefer to stay with them at home or indeed cannot find suitable child-care facilities. Another factor is that some Greek-Cypriot women who have been brought up in a Cypriot village find it very difficult to make the transition into the 'normal' work situation, travelling to work and being able to cope with the relationships at work which are often dominated by gossip.   Those women who are homeworkers and have small children have often to work from early in the morning to late evening to make a reasonable wage or to finish 'the lot' for the supplier to collect at a specific time.   Some women are also so driven by the desire to make as much money as they can, often to be able to buy a house, or buy land or build in Cyprus, or even to buy new furniture (a 'luxurious' house in the 'Cypriot' idiom being always sought) that they exert themselves at great cost to themselves and their children.   Often the piece-rate they are on is so low - for example a summer dress can be as little as 50 pence - that they really do work 'all' day to make a reasonable wage.   Their children in that case are often left to themselves, perhaps being taken out only for shopping, and often the hazards of sewing machine and iron are attendant on their play.   The sewing machine may be located in the kitchen with its other hazards of cooking and, in the winter, the presence of an electric or paraffin heater.   We do not possess data on the language development of such children but indications are that they start school with two disadvantages. Firstly they may not be able to speak English and secondly they have lacked stimulating play activity and their general

aptitude is underdeveloped.　The provision of pre-school
nursery facilities for such children is vital for two reasons.
One is to allow the mother more choice in the type of work
she undertakes and the other is to allow her children opportunities for the language development often denied them.
The pressures on a Cypriot woman to earn money and at the
same time to fulfil her household and child-care obligations,
often under the extraordinary demands of a patriarchal male
authority who expects his 'Cypriot' meals (usually time-con-
suming to prepare), are tremendous.

Sexual divisions, migration and economic independence

The subservience of the female within her economic role to
her husband, brother or father helps us to understand in
part the way in which the incorporation of women into economic production failed to transform sexual divisions.　That is
not to deny that women 'gained' certain advantages and freedom.　Where women worked, they could contribute their own
wages to providing a home and thus regarded the house
bought as a joint property.　Women often boasted of their
money and how much they made as machinists - some being
able to find employment more easily than their men.　Even
though in the sphere of sexual role definition more broadly
conceived, this had little effect (one would have been sur-
prised if it had), none the less it provided women with more
'clout' as far as sexual politics were concerned.　For example
an issue that many women were forced to confront when they
initially came over was their husband's pursuit of English
women who were willing to enter into sexual relations without
the need for life-long commitment.　Some men had even
established long-term on-going relations with another woman.
Cypriot women were more able to refuse to countenance such
situations given their economic contribution than if they were
totally economic dependants.

Another offshoot of women's economic contribution was to increase the 'cash-nexus' of the Cypriot woman.　A significant
characteristic of the Cypriot male migrant is that he has a
high degree of economic orientation to his country of settlement alongside a particular orientation to his country of origin.
Often economic success is sought as an attempt to improve his
status within the class system in Cyprus and within the fairly
self-contained Greek-Cypriot community in London.　The
woman, who if she does not work, often argues that her home
and children are more important than money, wishes to accumulate more once she is engaged in wage work, often insisting
that this is her money rather than ours (this is linked to
women's legal possession of property in Cyprus via the house-
dowry form).　This economic motivation of the woman begins
as a necessity of subsistence but may also involve a competi-

tive and consumption-oriented social display. The Greek-Cypriot life-style in London is directed to the Greek-Cypriot community in Cyprus and London and emphasises conspicuous consumption - property ownership, large car ownership, big spending and lavish furnishings. The main difference between the 'Hendon' and the 'Haringey' Greek-Cypriot is that the first is more economically successful - more likely to own his own business than the second; cultural and other attendant characteristics of 'class' position are often missing. Certain suburbs of London are designated as status areas, like Hendon, Finchley and Barnet. Those who live in Hackney are more likely to live in council flats - those in the suburbs in 1930s semi-detached villas. It is women's exploited but often lucrative work that contributes to the social move from one area to a 'better' one.

Greek-Cypriot men still expect their wives to be solely responsible for child care and domestic labour even when they work full-time, overtime and receive reasonable wages. A woman can bring in a net pay of £80-£100 per week for machining although the good days are now over and women have had to take a wage-cut. She may return home exhausted, tend her children and her husband, do her housework and shopping and then collapse into bed. It is not surprising then that women are some of the most dissatisfied members of the community and suffer from ailments and depressions so frequently. Men on the other hand when they finish work (although it must be said that they too work long hours, and if they have a small business in the evenings and weekends) can enjoy the cafe society or clubs that are a masculine domain, such as exist in the Finsbury Park area of Haringey. They go there to 'retreat' from their family and 'rediscover' the male life-style of their homeland. Older women may serve in these cafes for they can no longer stand as 'sexual' beings but most women do not enter these cafes.

Despite the dissatisfactions of Cypriot women they rarely see any other alternatives open for them. For example in a recent study conducted by the Haringey Area Management Team, Greek-Cypriot women had a much lower than average desire to 'retrain'. (4) The definition they have of themselves is as wives and mothers first and work is for cash, not the performance of a rightful role. They do not conceptualise themselves as 'legitimate' workers with aspirations for careers and improvement. They often visualise a period when these problems will be solved by returning to the 'homeland' (the 'Patrida'), although many I have spoken to see their roots in Cyprus being steadily eroded, saying it would be nice for holidays, not to live - 'we belong here now, we made our choice earlier on.'

Notions of women's sexuality have remained largely unchanged within the British setting, parents stressing the need for 'virginity' and frowning upon 'boyfriends'. There exists a

tension therefore between these traditional Greek-Cypriot
sexual mores and behaviour and those of British society and
this often expresses itself in the relations between parents
and their daughters.   During the 1960s, especially, there
was debate in the Greek-Cypriot press in London and in the
ethnic schools how best to deal with this.   The opportunities for struggle against patriarchal control are greater in
London for various reasons.   Firstly, girls and women are
not so closely supervised as in the villages and towns in
Cyprus, the younger women especially who are more likely to
take clerical and secretarial work in non-Cypriot establish-
ments.   Secondly, parents are often particularly anxious
about the public display of sexual behaviour, concerned about
'what will they think of us', and tend not to be so pristinely
traditionalist in the larger and more anonymous environment
of London or the other large cities in which Cypriots have
settled.   Thirdly, girls and women are subjected to a set of
different norms and practices in relation to female sexuality
and may have been at school introduced to debates concerning
women's rights, equality, sexuality and feminism.   Thus they
are more 'prepared' for a struggle with their parents.   What
is noticeable however is the degree to which girls 'manage'
the dissonance they thus encounter.   Most Greek-Cypriot
girls do not openly flout their parents' expectations, but all
indications show that they are more likely in private, secret-
ly, to entertain different attitudes and behaviour.   Greek-
Cypriot girls often have boyfriends and some (a minority) may
have full sexual relations with them - parents may suspect
but as long as public display has not taken place and as long
as they are assured in their own minds that the girl is still a
virgin they make concessions.   Of course it is difficult to
make a general rule and clearly parental attitudes vary.   But
we argue that some easing of the material expression of the
ideology of sexual purity has taken place and that women in
England have more freedom and are provided with more opportunities to exercise their independent judgment.
  In addition the material reality of the oppression by the
dowry-house has largely disappeared.   A common practice is
that parents will provide financial help with setting up a home.
Those who are well-off may provide a house on their daughter's marriage.   But this is an added bonus for the bride
and groom and not mandatory.   Arranged marriages are less
common in London than Cyprus although they are still the
'norm'.   Marriage is no longer a clear economic transaction
although often economic considerations weigh into the choice
of marriage partner for both men and women.   Women also
have the opportunity to marry a non-Cypriot which a small
minority do, preferring Englishmen to members of other ethnic
minority groups.   Parents will violently disapprove but eventually reconcile themselves to the 'reality', especially once
such a relationship has been on public display.   Most Greek-

Cypriot girls and boys I have spoken to would prefer to
marry another Greek-Cypriot and most in theory maintain the
notion of female 'honour' as mandatory.   However, material
circumstances as they become older may transform the actual
expression of these notions.

What is particularly marked about Greek-Cypriot girls is
that once leaving school they revert to a more Greek-Cypriot
environment, maintaining only their Greek-Cypriot school-
friends and increasingly devoting their leisure to the pursuit
of Greek-Cypriot activities.   It appears to be in their economic interests to maintain these, since Greek-Cypriot parents
have an ideology of 'sacrifice' towards their children that not
only imbues guilt but also self-interest.   Girls are often provided with cars, clothes and food and allowed to keep their
wage-packet.   They have also been brought up to submit to
parental will and once they are defined as 'grown-up' and not
so fully dependent they do it as their obligation.   However,
we do not want to underestimate the 'strictness' of some
fathers.   A further factor is that often the geographical
social, economic and political links of the Greek-Cypriot community act as effective 'policing' mechanisms.   Greek-
Cypriots congregate in particular areas, many of them working there and having a close network of family and relatives.
Under such conditions, traditional sexual relations and roles
are preserved.   Parents have also provided an example of
ethnic insularity for most have little contact with English
neighbours or work-mates and Greek-Cypriot girls are discouraged or often forbidden from 'going out' with English
girlfriends.   Greek-Cypriots have a low view of English
women, regarding them as polluted and they do not wish their
daughters to associate with them for fear of contamination.
Greek-Cypriot men are especially condemnatory of English
women although they are often themselves willing to have
sexual relations with them when the opportunity presents
itself.

Despite some progressive effects of migration on women,
such as the growth of economic independence and the decline
of the arranged marriage and the dowry, indications are that
the women's subordination to male authority is still great.
Firstly, despite the reasonable wages many women make as
machinists, women have little security or power in their work,
their hours of work or conditions.   Secondly, women will not
actively struggle against their husbands and risk estrange-
ment.   Separated or divorced women are often distressed in
the social setting of the Cypriot dress factory where most are
forced to work - abused by men and gossiped about by women
because the 'normal' unit for Cypriot society is the nuclear
patriarchal unit.   There are no possible alternative life-styles
available for any women within the Cypriot idiom in London,
since they often barely speak English and/or have no social
contacts with English people.   It is unlikely that they could

find the support for struggle against their husbands from
within the Cypriot community and may not know of any English groups who might help.   Without the family the whole
fabric of social life would collapse, especially for older women
whose parents are in Cyprus and who have no relatives of
their own in England.   Their friends are likely to be 'family'
friends for Greek-Cypriot women of the older generation
rarely have 'individual' friends.   Despite this, indications
show a greater 'willingness' of Cypriot women to separate or
seek divorces from their husbands than in Cyprus.

In terms of the quality of life, Cypriot migrant women
suffer increased isolation away from the familiar and closely-
knit community of the village or small town in Cyprus in the
large urban setting of London.   Child care is more difficult
in London where women work, the older mother or relatives
are not available to such an extent to care for children.
Leisure is reduced as both men and women are driven by the
desire to survive, and save, possibly for an eventual return
to Cyprus.

Whereas men can 'escape' at times from the burdens of loneliness and weariness to the masculine domain of the cafe or
club, women have no escape whether they work at home or in
the factory.   Greek-Cypriot women have gained some economic independence but often this has been at great personal
and social cost to themselves.   However, those women who
choose not to work while their children are small do not even
have some economic independence as a palliative to their isolated and oppressed existence.

CONCLUSIONS

We have argued the central role of the economic participation
of women in the constitution of the ethnic economy.   We have
also shown the particular problems they face in the context of
the clothing industry which often involves the extension of
the patriarchal relations of the Greek-Cypriot family in the
sphere of work.

Greek-Cypriot 'adaptation' to British society has been one
whereby ethnicity has been used as a resource for achieving
the economistic aims of migration.   When Greek-Cypriots
migrate they do so for economic reasons and see their stay in
England as 'instrumental' in achieving a better standard of
living for themselves and their children.   Unlike West Indians
for example they 'knew' what to expect of the British - they
did not think that they would be 'welcomed' with open arms.
Their experience of anti-colonialist struggle and the 'atroci-
ties' of the British in the EOKA period were clear evidence of
this. (5)   They came expecting to work and had a 'will to
succeed'.   Self-employment was the path that a significant
number took and some were indeed successful.   Even these

however had to sacrifice personal life and leisure.   The rest
often worked for Cypriot employers.   A situation developed
whereby migrants were exploiting migrants, in order to
achieve their economistic aims in a naturally difficult sphere
(the small concerns and vulnerability of the clothing and
catering sectors).   For employees 'ethnic' employment gave
them opportunities they were excluded from otherwise through
lack of language and low educational qualifications.   Employers used ethnic ties and family ties in the process of
social 'advancement'.   Women were both the mainstay of this
advancement (it was their labour that facilitated the 'ethnic'
economy) and have borne the brunt of it.   On the other
hand, women too migrated usually for economic reasons - to
work.   The conditions of wage-labour in Britain have not
led, in an unambiguous fashion, to their economic independence.   Cypriot women in London suffer a 'triple burden',
as women, as migrants and as workers for migrant men.   On
the other hand the younger ones are experiencing opportunities for the mitigation of the oppression by the traditional
Greek-Cypriot family as they learn to manage the cultural
moral and sexual contradictions they face.

NOTES

1 This paper arises out of a larger piece of research on
   Greek-Cypriot ethnicity and class in Britain.   For the
   discussion here the most important research methods were
   participant observation and intensive interviews.   Five
   clothing factories were visited regularly on a 'friendly'
   basis over a period of two years as I had relatives and
   friends working in them.   I also interviewed forty women
   in their homes, either with a tape-recorder or taking extensive notes; twenty-five of these women were clothing
   workers.   Leaders and representatives of the community
   were also interviewed and groups of young people were
   talked to at various Greek-Cypriot centres.   I also
   belonged to a Greek-Cypriot women's organisation and a
   women's group.   Data collected by Haringey were consul-
   ted and special analyses done of the Greek-Cypriot constit-
   uent of the Haringey Child-Care Survey in West Green.
2 My own calculations are based on the 1971 census and the
   CRE Report (1979).   Other estimates vary between 120,000
   to 140,000 (e.g. see R. Oakley, 1979).
3 Cypriots are included under the category of 'European New
   Commonwealth' in the 1971 census, along with Malta, Gozo
   and Gibraltar.   There is no differentiation here between
   Greek-Cypriots and Turkish-Cypriots.   These figures
   therefore must only be viewed as an approximation.
4 My own analysis of the data collected.   See Haringey Area
   Management Team (1981).

5 The EOKA liberation struggle took place in Cyprus
   between 1955 and 1959 and culminated in the granting of
   'independence' in 1960.   This gave Britain a continuing
   military presence and gave rights of intervention to
   Britain, Greece and Turkey.   See F. Anthias and R.
   Ayres (1979) for a discussion of this curtailed independence and the effects of the EOKA struggle.

5 In the front line

Annie Phizacklea

In focusing attention on the class position of migrant women workers in advanced industrial Western Europe we do more than render them 'visible' as a category of workers. The vast majority of migrant women from the European periphery and the Third World can be described as working class, by virtue of the fact that they sell their labour power for a wage and are predominantly located in semi- and unskilled manual jobs. Nevertheless their objective position within that class is determined by their specific position within economic, politico-legal and ideological relations, factors which underpin complex racial and sexual divisions within the working class. To act as though migrant women were peripheral to Western European class structure (see Morokvasic's critique of extant literature) is to lend support to those forces which act to fragment and weaken the working class internationally.

In the analysis which follows I have chosen to examine the position of migrant women workers from the European periphery and the Third World in the British, French and West German social formations. I set out with one main question: do all such women occupy the same objective position within the class structure, or put differently, are they part of the same racially and sexually categorised fraction of the working class? In answering that question I will examine migrant women's position in politico-legal and ideological relations and then go on to consider their position in economic relations. In the final part of this chapter I want to consider what lessons can be learnt from the self-organisation and struggle of migrant women workers in the three countries chosen for comparison.

A number of accounts have indicated that migrant labour generally occupies a subordinate position in economic, politico-legal and ideological relations in Western Europe (Castles and Kosack, 1973; Castells, 1975; Nikolinakos, 1975). And it has been argued elsewhere that we can in fact see the operation of a self-fulfilling prophecy: migrant labour, having been 'produced' by the demand for labour in socially undesirable and low-wage sectors of the economy, is confined to those sectors, often by specific policies and practices which are partially justified by the ascription of inferior characteristics, the consequence then being viewed as vindication of the ideology (Phizacklea and Miles, 1980, p. 14). Here, I will consider the policies and practices first and then go on to consider the labour market function of migrant women.

95

MIGRANT WOMEN AND POLITICO-LEGAL AND IDEOLOGICAL RELATIONS

With the exception of Castles's and Kosack's (1973) pioneering study, the bulk of research on migrant labour in Britain has been cast within a 'race relations' framework focusing on a settler population from colonial regions.   In contrast research in mainland Europe has primarily focused attention on a supposedly temporary guestworker population.   Not only is this distinction analytically misleading.   It takes no account of developments in policy over the last fifteen years. The most important development in the sphere of politico-legal relations is in my view the convergence of immigration policy throughout Western Europe and the establishment of a contradictory 'dual policy'.   What this means is that since 1974 virtually all advanced industrial Western European countries have heavily controlled or simply halted the entry of any new workers from outside the confines of the European Community. The other side of the dual policy is to introduce measures aimed at the 'integration' of those foreigners allowed to stay, with particular emphasis on the second generation.   Britain established this 'dual policy' ten years earlier than the other labour importing countries in Western Europe so that the inherent contradictions in the policy have been quite clear to an observer of the British situation for some time.

The first lesson to be learnt from the British situation is that by banning the further entry of certain categories of workers, those workers are officially stamped 'unwanted surplus'.   Whatever the measures that are subsequently introduced to 'aid the integration' of the same category of workers and their families already resident, they have been officially defined as a problem and become prime candidates for scapegoating (Miles and Phizacklea, 1979).

Second, immigration control has the effect of turning temporary migration into permanent settlement (Castles, 1980a). Why that happens is fairly obvious.   If a worker belongs to a category which becomes subject to immigration control, the problems of legal re-entry (even after a holiday) can be difficult or impossible.   In these circumstances staying put and sending home for the family, where circumstances permit, is like taking out an insurance policy in the face of an uncertain future.   But because this result of immigration control is unintended by the state, it expends considerable energy in reminding migrants of their insecure position.   Tactics include regarding all migrants as possible illegal entrants (Wilson, 1978;   Institute of Race Relations, 1979), deportation (Migrants' Action Group, 1981), ensuring that family re-unification is as difficult as possible (Moore and Wallace, 1975; Dummett, 1976), and defining the second generation as a 'law and order' problem (Hall et al., 1978).

The same contradictions are now quite clearly established

throughout mainland Western Europe. Before moving on to these developments in France and West Germany I will give a very schematic account of the history of labour migration in Britain and the differing mechanisms of control which have operated over different categories of migrant labour. In Britain there are two basic mechanisms of control over migrant labour which ensures its subordinate position in politico-legal relations. First, there is the category of 'alien' (foreigner) subjected to the work permit system, tied to specific work and denied political rights. Such workers occupy a de jure subordinate position in politico-legal relations. Second, there are black workers from the New Commonwealth who until 1962 had, as Commonwealth citizens, the right to live and work in Britian without restriction and, until the implementation of the 1971 Immigration Act, did not have the legal status of alien. Thus all such migrants who arrived prior to the legislative changes had and continue to have the same de jure politico-legal rights as the indigenous population, except for the right of certain dependants to live with them (Moore and Wallace, 1975). Nevertheless despite legislation outlawing racial discrimination, black migrants and their children in Britain continue to experience widespread discrimination in employment, housing and the provision of services (Smith, 1977; Hubbuck and Carter, 1981; see also Dex's chapter in this volume). These migrants do not formally occupy a subordinate position in politico-legal relations, but do so in a de facto sense. There are other groups of migrant labour such as the Cypriots and the Irish whose position in politico-legal relations is somewhat different. Cypriots, also originating from the New Commonwealth, have in law the same status as black migrant labour, nevertheless there is little doubt that they do not continue to experience widespread racial discrimination. Migrant labour from Ireland is not subject to legal restriction (provisions were made for such restriction in 1962 though they have never been enforced), though the Irish have historically been subject to racial discrimination in Britain (Miles, 1982).

Over the last 150 years these differing mechanisms of control have acted as a major contributory factor in confining migrant labour, particularly women, to the socially undesirable and low-wage sectors of the British labour market. In the nineteenth century it was Irish women, who escaped hunger and possibly death to work as domestics in British households (Redford, 1976). Later came official recruitment of Irish women for domestic work in homes and hospitals (Department of Employment, 1976), their numbers supplemented in the immediate post-war period by Italian women and European volunteer workers. By 1947, 65 per cent of all work permits issued, were for domestic service (over 90 per cent of domestics are women; Hakim, 1978). In the late 1950s and the 1960s Irish and Italian women were joined in predominantly

service work by rapidly increasing numbers of Spanish and,
to a lesser extent, Portuguese women (MacDonald and Mac-
Donald, 1972).   But the late 1950s and 1960s also saw the
entry of large numbers of West Indian and Cypriot women
into British labour markets (Phizacklea, 1982 and Anthias in
this volume) to be joined at a slightly later date by women
from Southern Asia.   While the vast majority of women
workers from the New Commonwealth are located in manual
work, they could not (and the vast majority still cannot) be
legally directed to specific types of work.   Thus Britain's
continuing need for domestic workers in hospitals, hotels and
private homes was reflected in special quotas being set aside
for the recruitment of foreign workers in these sectors until
1979.   Filipino and Malaysian women took up the largest
share of new entries in these sectors during the 1970s.

The history of migrant labour in France and the mechanisms
of control which have operated over it bear obvious parallels
with the British experience.   First, both countries have
drawn on colonial and ex-colonial labour as well as labour
from the European periphery.   Second, while the Office
National d'Immigration was set up in 1945 to officially organise
the recruitment of labour, the greatest part of labour migration up to 1974 was, like Britain, not officially organised
(Castles and Kosack, 1973).   Third, just as Britain moved,
during the 1960s and 1970s, to ban immigration from ex-colonial countries with predominantly black populations and to deny
these populations rights of citizenship, France has acted in a
similar manner towards migrants from her former colonies in
North and Central Africa (Wisnewski, 1979; Costa-Lascoux,
1980).   But the parallels between Britain and France go further.   Following the ban on new worker entries to France in
1974, a succession of ministerial decrees were enacted prohib-
iting the entry of family members to the labour market and
introducing repatriation schemes and measures aimed at increasing surveillance of resident migrants (Costa-Lascoux,
1980).   The contradictions in France's dual policy are highlighted in the following statement: 'Although integration policies are developing (on lines that do not exclude the maintenance of links with the original culture) and are becoming more
democratic...the French government still pursues its policy of
repatriation aid' (SOPEMI, 1980, p. 95).   While a number of
the most repressive decrees have subsequently been annulled
by the Conseil d'Etat (for instance the ban on family members'
labour-market entry) and the new Socialist administration in
France is pledged to giving migrants a 'fairer deal', what this
means in practice has yet to be demonstrated.   Finally there
is one major difference between the attitude to immigration in
France as compared to Britain or West Germany.   France has
declared itself a country of 'immigration' and has historically
encouraged family re-unification in line with its desire for
population growth.

In contrast, West Germany still maintains it is not a country of immigration and consistent with *this* view organised a highly efficient system of rotating migration from the late 1950s onwards. Bilateral agreements were made with countries viewed as culturally close and yet which had no direct colonial tie with West Germany (and whose citizens therefore had no residual claims to citizenship). Agreements were made with Italy (1955), Greece and Spain (1960), Turkey (1961), Portugal (1964) and with Yugoslavia (1968). Recruiting agencies were set up in each country to match man and woman power with labour requirements in West Germany. From the millions of applicants, agencies could afford to be highly selective in their recruitment criteria. Family reunification was actively discouraged and until the official ban on immigration in 1973 the majority of migrant women in West Germany had entered as workers rather than as dependants.

Nevertheless the whole system of rotating migration (see Introduction) showed signs of breaking down as early as the 1966-7 recession in West Germany. While many thousands of migrants were forced to leave the country due to unemployment many rode out the recession claiming whatever unemployment benefit they were entitled to. In addition competition for migrant labour increased throughout the 1960s between labour importing countries. As bilateral and multilateral agreements were renewed, West Germany (along with other countries) was forced to concede the right of workers to be joined by their families (Castles, 1980a). Nevertheless there never has been any concomitant right of spouses and dependants to automatic entry into the labour market. Currently children must wait two years and spouses four before they can gain a work permit, which is subject to the precedence of Germans and nationals of the European Community. Only young people with five years' residence and with one parent with five years' employment in West Germany can gain a work permit which is not subject to this precedence (SOPEMI, 1980). This does however constitute an improvement on the previous situation.

Thus recent West German policy aims to make entry into the labour market and naturalisation easier for the second generation, presumably in an effort to defuse the threat of what is commonly referred to as the 'social time bomb' (Castles, 1980b). Nevertheless West Germany introduced 'repatriation assistance' in 1982, highlighting the contradictions in its 'dual policy'. Only naturalisation can bring de jure civil and political equality for migrants. But even if de jure equality were established in the sphere of politico-legal relations, the British experience indicates that racism, which in the present political and economic conjuncture appears to have become widespread throughout Western Europe, can subordinate as effectively as the plethora of regulations, visas and permits used to control 'foreign' migrant labour.

Up to this point I have made very few distinctions between
the position of male and female migrants in politico-legal relations.   While there are clear cases of sexual discrimination in
immigration policy, which work to perpetuate women's subordination to, and dependency on, men (see Amrit Wilson, 1978,
for the British case) what is equally significant are the
effects of immigration control on the politico-legal position of
female migrants and the way in which regulations are adminis-
tered.   To reiterate, because the great majority of 'spouses'
allowed to join workers under regulations permitting family re-
unification remain women, then it is they and their children
who take the full brunt of the administration of immigration
control.   If family re-unification is a 'right' in Britain,
France and West Germany for the more long-standing migrant
worker's families, then it is a very perverse type of 'right'.
In practice it means immigration control differentially applied
to different categories of people.   Once a category of
workers have been stamped with the 'unwanted' label then
every obstacle and indignity will be put in the path of families wishing to join them (World Council of Churches, 1980).
There is plenty of evidence in the British case to show how
this works.   In 1962, the entry of workers from the New
Commonwealth (whose populations are mainly black) was
heavily restricted, but the families of workers already resident still had the right to come to Britain.   While migration
from the West Indies had by this time achieved something
approaching an equalisation of sex ratios, migration from the
Indian subcontinent was still heavily weighted in favour of
men.   As the apparatus of institutionalised racism was
strengthened through subsequent immigration acts (1968 and
1971) so too was the level of discrimination in the administration of that legislation.   There have been cases of women
who had the correct documentary evidence necessary for entry
being subjected to 'virginity tests', their children's bones X-
rayed, 'to prove' that they really were the people that their
documentation proved (Wilson, 1978).   Women from the New
Commonwealth who had the right to live and work in Britain
without restriction but who had left an 'illegitimate' child
behind in the care of relatives (and this applied to thousands
of West Indian women) have to prove they have had
'sole' responsibility for the child's welfare and upbringing
during the mother's absence if they were to be re-united and
this rule has been harshly applied by Immigration Appeal
Tribunals (Hewitt, 1976).   Women who had been allocated
resident domestic work permits and who had not declared,
because they had not been asked, that they had dependent
children under the age of sixteen in their homeland, were
declared illegal entrants and 'removed' from the country when
they asked if their children could come and join them
(Migrants' Action Group, 1981).   To reiterate, resident domestic work permits were abolished in 1979, up until that point

the Filipino women who had taken up the largest share of
entries in this category were welcomed as 'willing workers'.
Then a regulation which was not intended as a method of
immigration control was used to reinterpret the law and
applied retrospectively in order to get rid of some of them.

The administration of immigration policy is only one area in
which migrant women occupy a subordinate position in politico-
legal relations and I believe we can only grasp why they
occupy that position by analysing their subordinate position
in ideological relations.   First, I believe a great deal of time
is wasted if one tries to answer the question 'which categories
of workers experience the greatest hostility?'   Or which
groups are racially categorised and which are not?   To reiterate, I believe that once a category of workers becomes
subject to tight immigration control then they are officially
stamped as unwanted and problematic and this applies irrespective of the colour, nationality or gender of the individual
migrant.   Having said this migrant women have a special
place in ideological relations because as women they are primarily defined as actual or potential wives and mothers and as
migrant women, 'illiterate, isolated...the bearers of many children' (Morokvasic in this volume).   I believe such views are
an important feature of the imperialist ideology which satu-
rates advanced industrial Western European culture and constitute a very basic element in contemporary racism as it
applies to women from economically dependent social formations.   As racism increases, the dominant stereotypes of
migrant women take on a special significance, with birth rates
constantly falling in Western Europe, we hear in France of 'a
dangerous isolation of ageing Europeans in an over-populated
world in which the Third World plays the card of natality'
(Michel Debre, 1979, quoted in Stolcke, 1981, p. 40).
Margaret Thatcher in Britain talks of people's fears of being
'swamped'.   Thus racism and sexism become intertwined in a
special way for migrant women.

I am arguing therefore that migrant women occupy a subordinate position in politico-legal and ideological relations and in
the next section I will argue that this position is replicated
and reinforced by their position in Western European labour
markets.

MIGRANT WOMEN AND ECONOMIC RELATIONS

In analysing the position of migrant women in economic relations we need answers to several questions: first, women
generally are constrained in their choice of work due to
sexual divisions within the labour market.   In these circumstances is it possible to argue that the entry of migrant women
into an already segregated labour market can introduce
another layer of segmentation?   Do migrant women occupy a

subordinate position within sectors of 'women's work'?
Second, it has been argued that women, generally and married women in particular (Beechey, 1978) and migrants
(Castles and Kosack, 1973) constitute a reserve army of
labour, to be brought in and thrown out of wage labour
according to the needs of capital.   Can women and migrants
generally be said to constitute a reserve army and in the
same way?   And where does this leave migrant women
workers?

In answering the first question I will examine levels of economic activity and the occupational distribution of migrant as
compared to 'indigenous' women in the three countries chosen
for comparison.   In response to the second question, I will
examine the unemployment rates for migrant as compared to
indigenous women and also to male unemployment rates wherever this is possible.

Comparisons of this type are fraught with difficulties and
given the problems of inadequate statistical bases, dated figures in the case of Britain (1971 census) and the overall
problem of comparing statistics which have been collected on
a different basis nationally, I offer what follows very tenta-
tively.   These problems are highlighted in the first exercise:
an examination of economic activity rates.   For example,
according to a British study carried out between 1972-5 only
16 per cent of Pakistani born women in Britain are engaged
in wage labour (Smith, 1977) yet according to a study carried out in Rochdale, most Pakistani women in that town are
homeworkers (Anwar, 1979).   This problem of under-enumer-
ation is particularly great in the case of migrant women who
have entered as 'spouses' and who either have no right of
automatic entry into the labour market, or who must wait for
a number of years before such entry is possible or who are
simply constrained from undertaking 'regular' work because
there is none available, because of child care or for religious
reasons.   We will return to the question of unregistered wage
work later, the point to be made here is that the following
figures should be treated as under-estimates.   In Britain,
persons born outside Britain constituted 5.6 per cent of the
total workforce in 1971.   In France they constitute 7.3 per
cent and in West Germany 9.5 per cent (SOPEMI, 1977-8).
In Britain and West Germany around a third of the migrant
workforce is female compared to only 19 per cent in France.

Economic activity rates also vary enormously by nationality,
for instance in Britain if we take married women workers aged
between thirty-five and forty-four years of age, according to
the 1977-8 National Dwelling and Housing Survey (NDHS) 88.5
per cent of West Indian women are economically active, 59.8
per cent of Indian women and 11.4 per cent of Pakistani and
Bangladeshi women.   The same differences in economic activity rates between groups of women can be found in France
and West Germany.   In France it is Yugoslavian women who

have the highest rates of economic activity (57 per cent) and
Italian and Tunisian women the lowest, 24 and 28.5 per cent
respectively (BELC, 1976).   In West Germany where the emphasis in immigration policy has been in favour of labour
migration as opposed to family migration, economic activity
rates amongst migrant women are across the board higher
than in France.   Thus in 1978, 66 per cent of Yugoslavian
women were recorded as economically active, 59 per cent of
Greek women, 54 per cent of Portuguese and 44 per cent of
Turkish women (Bundesansalt für Arbeit, 1980).

When we turn to occupational distribution, we must rely in
the British case on a very dated statistical source (the 1971
census) if we want to accurately examine the occupational distribution of all women compared to the women born outside the
United Kingdom.   Table 5.1 sets out the occupational distribution of migrant women and working women generally.

TABLE 5.1   *Occupational distribution of migrant and working
women generally in selected industries, Britain 1971*

	NC	Irish	Non-EEC Europe	OC	All non-UK	All women
Engineering and allied trades	6.9	5.2	3.3	0.5	5.0	3.2
Clothing	9.8	1.8	6.1	0.5	5.6	3.6
Clerical	16.2	16.3	14.0	38.1	17.0	27.2
Sales workers	2.5	6.2	6.7	4.6	5.4	11.6
Service	15.9	33.2	33.6	9.7	25.5	22.3
Professional	20.9	18.1	14.1	36.8	19.2	11.7

Source: 1971 Census of Population, Special tabulation
DT 1746 and Economic Activity Table Part II in Department of
Employment, 1976, p. 121.
Key: NC = New Commonwealth;   OC = Old Commonwealth;
All non-UK = all countries outside UK;   All women = all eco-
nomically active females.

These census categories must be treated with some caution on
a number of counts.   First, the category 'New Commonwealth'
includes for instance white women born in Pakistan and India.
Second, the professional category includes nursing.   While
no breakdown was available for the 1971 census, we do know
that in 1966, 77.5 per cent of Caribbean women in Greater
London and 99 per cent in the West Midlands listed as profes-
sionals were nurses (Rose, 1969, pp. 161-2).   This same
concentration in nursing applies also to Irish, Malaysian,
Mauritian, Filipino and West African women.   While I do not

question the 'professional' status of nursing (though nurses themselves would argue that their pay bears little relation to that status), there is official evidence to suggest that immigrant women are over-represented in the least desirable sectors of nursing (Department of Employment, 1976).

What is quite clear from this distribution is that unless a migrant woman originates from the 'Old Commonwealth' (which means the white Commonwealth, Australia, New Zealand, Canada, etc.) she is less likely than women born in the United Kingdom to be located in those sectors of 'women's' work which have expanded rapidly since the last war. Thus migrant women are over-represented in certain manufacturing industries (instrument and electrical engineering, vehicles, metal goods, clothing, leather and footwear), in nursing and in the manual sectors of the service industries.

Having said this different categories of women have undoubtedly had different functions within the labour market. Work permit holders, particularly from Southern Europe and South-East Asia, are more likely to be located in manual service jobs, than women originating from the New Commonwealth. But Irish women also are over-represented in these sectors which is highly significant given the 150 year history of female labour migration from Ireland. Irish labour is not subject to the work permit system and remains unaffected by the succession of immigration laws passed in Britain since 1962. And yet Irish women more than any other group play what we can term a permanent female migrant worker role within British labour markets.

On the basis of occupational distribution it is possible to suggest that whether or not a migrant woman originating from the European periphery or the Third World in Britain is subject to the work permit system, whether she is black or white, she is likely to be located in the manual sectors of 'women's' work or in sectors of 'professional women's' work suffering from acute labour shortages, such as nursing and allied medical services. To this extent there is a relatively high degree of occupational crowding within an already sexually divided labour market.

According to the 1975 census in France the same broad distinctions between migrant and indigenous women's occupational distribution can be found in French labour markets. While 30 per cent of foreign women are located in 'non-market' services (e.g. domestics) less than 1 per cent of indigenous French women are to be found in these jobs. At the other extreme is the under-representation of foreign women in the expanding 'white blouse' sectors of economic activity, with 27 per cent of French women employed in banking, insurance, etc., against 1 per cent of foreign women (Samman, 1977).

But census statistics present a very static picture of what is actually going on within women's employment overall. The means for building a dynamic picture are supplied in statistics

compiled by Singer-Kerel (1980).   Using a number of different sources, census statistics, surveys of foreign manpower
and the employment surveys carried out by INSEE, it is possible to indicate a number of broad trends effecting foreign
women's employment in France.

First in terms of the rate of penetration or the share of
foreign women in a given socio-economic category, in the
period 1962-75, foreign women's share of unskilled work rose
sharply.   Thus while for example the number of foreign
women in domestic service declined slightly, the actual proportion of foreign domestics increased (Singer-Kerel, 1980,
pp. 56-7 and Table 3c).

Second, the ratio of skilled to unskilled labour for French
and foreign men and women changed dramatically between
1962 and 1975, see Table 5.2.   While the 'de-skilling' of

TABLE 5.2   *Ratio of skilled to unskilled labour in France*

	Women		Men	
	Foreign	Total population	Foreign	Total population
1962	41.8	44.3	56.0	95.4
1968	32.2	43.4	45.5	92.3
1975	19.2	23.1	54.1	101.8

Source: INSEE, Enquetes Emploi, Recensements, compiled by
Singer-Kerel, 1980, p. 74.

foreign women has been dramatic over this period, it is significant that women workers generally have met the same fate.
These figures illustrate the continuing struggle being fought
over the 'skill' label, resulting in the 'sexualisation of skill
labels following the actual de-skilling of work processes'
(Phillips and Taylor, 1980, p. 85).   Skill is thus defined
against women.

The West German situation provides further evidence of
migrant women's subordinate position in economic relations.
In terms of occupational distribution, in June 1979 57 per cent
of migrant women (including nationals of the EEC) were located in manufacturing jobs as compared to 29 per cent of all
working women in West Germany (Bundesanstalt für Arbeit,
1980).   A decade earlier, June 1969, 70 per cent of foreign
women were located in manufacturing, thus there has been a
noticeable shift into the tertiary sector during this ten-year
period, though not into the 'white blouse' sectors.   In 1969,
6.3 per cent of foreign women were located in banking, insur-
sance, etc., yet in 1979 only 1.2 per cent of foreign women
were located in these sectors.   In contrast the percentage
employed in hotels and catering has risen rapidly.

In sectors of manufacturing industry experiencing consider-

able decline in employment over this ten-year period, such as
clothing, the rate of penetration of foreign women has increased.   But this also applies to expanding industries such as
chemicals.   Singer-Kerel's conclusion that migrant workers
in France have been used to both preserve the old and build
the new is, I believe, equally applicable to the West German
case, though it might be more appropriate to suggest 'servic-
ing' the new in the case of foreign women.

The question of skill status is more difficult to analyse in
the West German case but it is possible to piece together a
similar trend to that observed for France.   Following the
1966-7 recession in West Germany the new round of recruitment in 1968 gave preference to women workers (Abadan-
Unat, 1977).   It is argued that the 'priority given female
immigrants stemmed from the advantages employers perceived
in maintaining large female work forces.... Employers thus
viewed migrant women workers as a reliable source of cheap
labour' (Kudat and Sabuncuoglu, 1980, pp. 14-15).   One can
only speculate about the type of re-organisation of jobs which
occurred during the recession, but it is likely that any 'new'
jobs for women in manufacturing were unskilled jobs.

Kudat's 1974 survey of Yugoslav and Turkish workers in
West Berlin indicated that while the majority of men and
women migrants were located in unskilled jobs upon arrival in
West Germany, within a few years there was a dramatic skill
improvement among the male migrant workers.   By 1974 only
29 per cent of Yugoslav men in her sample were employed as
unskilled workers, compared to 94 per cent of the women
(Kudat and Sabuncuoglu, 1980, pp. 15-16).

Thus in terms of occupational distribution migrant women
originating from the Third World or the European periphery
occupy a subordinate position within British, French and West
German labour markets.   I believe that their concentration
within the manual sectors of 'women's' work does in fact represent a new layer of segmentation within these labour markets.   Migrant men have experienced some advance in terms
of skill level which has not been shared by their female
counterparts.   But to argue that indigenous women have
gained in occupational status at the expense of their migrant
counterparts is, I believe, a debatable point.   Over the last
twenty years both indigenous and migrant women have been
shifting from manufacturing industries into the tertiary or
service sector.   But whereas indigenous women were moving
in ever greater numbers into more 'desirable' low pay 'white
blouse' jobs, migrant women have been moving from one form
of low-pay manual job to another, or to the lowest ranks of
non-manual work.   Nevertheless, 'desirability' in this case is
based on the notion that non-manual work is of higher status
than manual work and that before the introduction of new
technology into the office more 'security' was offered by the
'white blouse' sectors (West, 1982).   But this line of argu-

ment leads us to the second question posed at the beginning
of this section; if migrant workers and women generally have
been conceptualised as a reserve army, where does this leave
migrant women? Are migrant women a more vulnerable section of the labour force than indigenous women? Are they a
specific type of reserve army of labour?

I believe that the answers to these questions are very complex and must take full account of the functions performed by
different categories of labour within Western European labour
markets. A reserve army of labour is not simply a body of
men and/or women who are brought in and thrown out of
wage labour according to cyclical fluctuations in capitalist
economies. A reserve army (defined in an orthodox Marxist
sense) must function as a competitor to those *in* work and
thereby weaken their position. Historically Irish migrant
labour in nineteenth-century Britain did act as a classic reserve army of labour and much of the conflict between the
newly emergent working class in Britain and Irish migrants
stemmed from the threat posed by the latter (Miles, 1982).
The point to be made is that the Irish were competitors of the
indigenous working class.

If we turn our attention to the position of women and
migrants in contemporary Western European labour markets I
believe we are analysing a very different situation. We are
examining labour markets where organised indigenous, male
labour has struggled to achieve a better position at the expense of weaker sections of labour, weaker in the sense that
they occupy a subordinate position in social relations prior
to their entry into the labour market. In the introduction to
this book we briefly discussed how this process works to
ghettoise women in gender specific and low paid sectors of
work. In the case of migrant labour the source of contemporary exclusionary practice within organised labour is rooted
in imperialism though the nature of the relationships involved
are the object of a good deal of debate (see Bonacich, 1980
for a useful overview). Some argue that the metropolitan
working class was literally 'bought off' with the profits of
Western European imperialist expansion and exploitation, the
latter justified by an ideology of racism alleging the innate
inferiority of the dominated. I have no quarrel with the
latter part of this argument; it is crucial to an understanding of contemporary forms of racism. But we must also consider the ways in which imperialism sets one group of workers
in competition with another, so that when migrant labour is
drawn from dominated social formations it is perceived by the
indigenous organised working class to pose a threat to hard
won gains. Thus when migrant labour arrives in the metropolitan society it is not met by the warm embrace of international brotherhood, but exclusionary practice (Miles and
Phizacklea, 1977 and 1978). Such practices act as one, albeit
important, element in the ghettoisation of migrant labour.

When we come to analyse the position of indigenous male
labour as compared to female labour and male and female
migrant labour we are therefore analysing the position of
relatively non-competitive groups.   In this respect, with the
rapidly increasing numbers of migrant women entering the
labour market, we can only begin to discuss their position as
a reserve army of labour in relation to themselves.

In what follows therefore I am asking a different question:
are some categories of labour more vulnerable to unemployment than others?   In considering female labour we should
in fact examine job loss not unemployment due to the high
level of unregistered unemployment amongst women.   For
example, it is estimated that half of the women who have lost
their jobs in the present recession in Britain are not registered as unemployed (Kellner, 1981).   Given the lack of
comparable official statistics on job loss in the three countries
chosen for comparison I must use the less satisfactory indica-
tor of recorded unemployment.

First there is evidence to show that unskilled workers are
the most vulnerable to unemployment during structural or
conjunctural crises (Smith, 1980 and Baudouin, Collin and
Guillerm, 1978).   Women generally are therefore more 'at
risk' because of their predominance in less skilled work.
Second in relation to Britain, Bruegel indicates that in situations where men and women are located in comparable work,
women are more vulnerable to job loss than men (1979).

The next rung in the hierarchy of vulnerability is to ascer-
tain whether migrant women are more vulnerable to unemployment than indigenous women.   While there are no unemployment statistics relating to migrant women generally in Britain,
the Department of Employment does record what it calls
'minority group' unemployment statistics.   Its analysis of unemployment levels during November 1973 to May 1975, a period
during which unemployment was rising overall, shows that the
proportionate increase in unemployment levels among minority
group women was nearly three times as large as among the
total female unemployed;   for minority men the increase was
twice as large as among the total male unemployed (DE, 1975,
p. 869).   When we move to a situation of 'all things being
equal' as described by Shirley Dex in this volume, we find
young black women last in the hiring queue and the first in
the firing queue.   In addition both Dex's and the DE's analyses indicate that when demand improves minority group women
are re-employed faster than women generally.

In France and West Germany we find a similar situation.
At the end of 1979 foreign women constituted 19 per cent of
the migrant labour force in France, but 31 per cent of the
unemployed foreigners.   In a year there had been a 21 per
cent proportionate increase of foreign women applying for
work, compared to 15 per cent for women generally, 7 per
cent for men generally and a reduction of 4 per cent among

foreign men (SOPEMI, 1980, pp. 70-1). Obviously the proportionate increase amongst foreign women job applicants has
to be assessed in the light of the rapidly increasing number
of foreign women seeking first-time access to the labour
market. Nevertheless the figures are an accurate record of
persons registering as unemployed and first-time access does
not account for the whole of this steep rise.

In the West German case, foreign women constituted 31.6
per cent of the foreign labour force on 30 September 1979,
but 49.3 per cent of the unemployed foreign work force
(SOPEMI, 1980, p. 79). While I have no corresponding figures for unemployment generally in West Germany at this
date, it is reported that the unemployment rate for foreigners
was higher than unemployment generally and that this discrepancy was on the increase (SOPEMI, 1980, p. 78).

While these figures take no account of unregistered unemployment, there is little doubt that migrant women are a more
vulnerable section of the workforce in terms of unemployment
than either their male counterparts or indigenous men and
women.

Having become wage-labourers in rapidly increasing numbers, the occupational distribution, sectoral mobility, the rate
of 'de-skilling', unemployment and re-employment patterns of
migrant women workers provides evidence of their subordinate position in economic relations. Combined with their
subordinate position in politico-legal and ideological relations I
believe that their objective position within the working class
is sufficiently distinct from that occupied by their male counterparts or indigenous men and women to warrant the description of a sexually and racially categorised class fraction.

There is one particular aspect of that class position which I
believe has not been subjected to the serious theoretical attention it deserves. This is the role of migrant women in the
process of class formation within migrant populations. There
is a very large literature on what is called 'middleman minorities' (see Bonacich and Modell, 1980, for a systematic cover-
age of this literature). It is a literature which focuses on
those migrant groups who have come to occupy a predominantly petit-bourgeois class position in many societies. A good
deal of attention is paid in this literature to the way in which
'resources' available within a specific ethnic group are used
to create alternative employment structures or a specific economic niche for migrants and 'their families'. I believe that
the major flaw in this literature is to play down or ignore the
fact that this petit-bourgeois class position can usually only
be achieved through the exploitation of other migrants, particularly female 'kith and kin'.

What is often called the 'ethnic economy' (see Anthias in this
volume for a further discussion) is seen to provide employment opportunities for migrants whose options are limited by
discrimination and in the case of women, the so-called disad-

vantages that they carry within them, including 'language
deficiencies', 'cultural preferences' and 'lack of recognised
skills'.   While such 'disadvantages' are part of the stereotype (see Morokvasic in this volume) and act as useful tools
for exploitation in the labour market generally, they play an
equally important part in the creation of the 'ethnic economy'.
In her study of small clothing workshops in Coventry, England, Barbro Hoel found that many of the Asian entrepreneurs shared the same stereotypical view of their Asian female
employees:

'I see the majority of women working for me as benefitting
from my job offer.   They are illiterate and have no skills,
hence no British factory will make use of them.... Their
£20 a week will help towards the family income, and we are
like a big family here' (Hoel, 1982, p. 86).

You can hear the same paternalism reflecting the incorporation
of pre-capitalist relations into a capitalist enterprise used to
justify exploitation in any city in contemporary Western
Europe.   And exploitation is in fact a necessity for the economic viability of the small-scale labour-intensive enterprise.
Self-employment is an escape route from badly paid, arduous,
unskilled manual work for many male migrants, yet with
meagre savings entrepreneurial projects which require a low
level of capital investment are the only possible options, and
include small-scale manufacturing, service and retail outlets.
Such projects are by definition, labour as opposed to capital
intensive and female relatives and friends constitute a supply
of cheap and flexible labour power.

In the final part of this chapter I want to shift the focus
away from migrant women's objective position within the class
structure to their role as active protagonists in class
struggle.   Earlier Morokvasic has argued that becoming a
wage labourer is an essential condition of migrant women
questioning at least some dimensions of their subordination.
I should quickly add that none of the contributors in this
book see wage labour as having some great liberating potential
for migrant women.   Rather it is the awareness of intensifi-
cation of oppression and exploitation through wage labour in
the migration setting which can have a liberating potential.

THE FIGHT BACK

'Management saw us as quiet Asian ladies who wouldn't
answer back.   Well we're going to show them what we can
do.'

The above quote comes from a conversation I recorded on the
second day of the dispute at Grunwick Film Processing Labor-
atories in north west London in August 1976.   Two years
later that dispute had gone down in labour history as repre-
senting a landmark in rank and file trade union solidarity and

yet for the migrant workers involved, mainly women, their two-year struggle to gain union recognition in their work-place ended in defeat, unemployment and a sense that they had eventually been betrayed by the trades union bureaucracy (Phizacklea and Miles, 1978).

Initially the dispute at Grunwick appeared to mark a turning point in the attitude and practice of British trades unions to the presence of migrant workers, particularly women. The record up to that point had at best been the neglect of issues concerning migrant workers, at worst, trade unions had been actively involved in discriminatory practice (Miles and Phizacklea, 1978). Whenever migrants have the opportunity of joining a trades union, they are not slow in doing so. Yet on many occasions when migrant workers have demonstrated their resistance to exploitation and reacted through self-organisation, formulating demands and taking strike action, trades unions have colluded with management in breaking those strikes. Clear cases of such action are the unofficial strike of Turkish workers at Ford's Cologne plant in 1973 (Castles and Kosack, 1974) and the following year at Imperial Typewriters Ltd in Britain, a strike initiated by migrant women (Miles and Phizacklea, 1978).

Migrant women have repeatedly demonstrated their resistance to the exploitation they experience in the workplace (for West Germany, see Kosack, 1976; for France, see Churches Committee on Migrant Workers, 1978 and Kudat and Sabancuoglu, 1980; for Britain, see Wilson, 1978; Hoel, 1982 and Phizacklea, 1982), and yet to date they have been marginalised by the very institutions of the labour movement which supposedly exist to protect and defend their interests as wage-labourers. Self-organisation and activity may have been forced on migrant women in the workplace but self-organisation is in itself a prerequisite for migrant women's struggle against their triple oppression. I have chosen in this chapter to concentrate on migrant women's position as wage-labourers but their subordinate position in the labour market is only one aspect of their overall fractionalised position within the working class. Many of the most pressing issues for migrant women are not over wages or degrading working conditions, they relate to basic human rights; the right to stay in the country, to be joined by their children, to have a decent place to live, to be free of racist harassment and violence. There is increasing evidence that migrant women are setting up their own organisations through which they can speak for themselves and articulate demands specific to their fractionalised class position (see CCMW, 1978, chapters 4 and 5 and Phizacklea, 1982). I am not suggesting that migrant women can 'go it alone', for moral and material support from outside their ranks is crucially important, but it has to be on their terms and around issues that are of importance to them. In conclusion I want to turn to the prospects

for migrant women as waged workers in Western Europe, a
future which I see as bleak.   As the economic crisis has
deepened in the advanced industrial countries of Western
Europe and as unemployment rises, so do the cries that
demand of women and migrants 'to go home'.   Despite considerable evidence 'that the opportunities for substitution
between foreign and national manpower are limited' (SOPEMI,
1980) and that male workers simply do not 'take over' whole
sectors of 'women's' work, the combined effects of the reloca-
tion of certain labour intensive manufacturing work and the
introduction of new technology are creating a surplus of
female and migrant labour.   As work in the formal economy
contracts, more and more workers, particularly women are
forced into the informal economy in search of insecure and
low paid work, often based in the home.   In her analysis of
the British clothing industry (an industry in which migrant
women are over-represented throughout Western Europe) Coyle
indicates that the rapid loss of jobs in the industry is not entirely due to increased efficiency and productivity, but to the
fact that some firms have chosen to move from factory production into the business of orchestrating the labour of homeworkers (Coyle, 1982, p. 18).

Finally the fact that migrant women constitute a reserve
army of labour in relation to themselves and that the number
of migrant women formerly registering themselves available
for waged work is increasing, means that employers have a
very powerful weapon with which to crush any attempts to
organise resistance to oppression and exploitation.   It is no
coincidence that in the last few years there have been less
industrial disputes initiated by migrant women.   The threat
of unemployment and the knowledge that there are other
migrant women who can be substituted for the same job, act
as deterrents to resistance amongst an already vulnerable
workforce.

In this chapter I have focused mainly on the position of
migrant women as workers.   To raise issues of housing, education, child care and health provision to name but a few of
the other areas in which migrant women are waging struggles
to combat discrimination and oppression would require another
chapter, if not another book.   To ignore such issues, to fail
to lend material support to them because they are viewed as
'marginal' to more wide-ranging attacks on working-class
rights and living standards is to adopt a 'head in the sand'
perspective.   Migrant women workers are very much a part
of the Western European working class, their issues are class
issues and to ignore them is to consciously lend support to
those who actively seek to weaken the working class internationally.

6 Living in between: Turkish women in their homeland and in the Netherlands

Lenie Brouwer and *Marijke Priester*

INTRODUCTION

'It seems to me that in Holland women have more authority
than men' forty-year-old man from Arpa.
Over the last ten years the number of Turkish women migrating to the Netherlands has rapidly increased. As feminist
anthropologists living in multi-racial Amsterdam we undertook
research which we hoped would make a contribution towards
bridging the gulf which currently exists between Dutch and
Turkish women who live alongside each other. (1)

Turkish women form the largest group of Mediterranean
women living in the Netherlands and alongside Yugoslavian
women have the highest rates of labour force participation. (2)   Our research interest developed through a Turkish friend who introduced us to many of the people from his
village now living in Amsterdam, all of whom came from
Arpa, (3) a village situated in the district of Konya, a very
religious part of Turkey.   Because we wanted to carry out
qualitative research we paid regular visits to ten women
within this larger village network.   In addition in order to
analyse the changes that the migration from Turkey to the
Netherlands has brought about for these women we undertook
two months fieldwork in Arpa itself.

Very little has been published about the specific effects of
migration on the position of women but a recurrent question
raised in the literature has been whether or not migration
leads to emancipation for women from rural areas.   We do not
intend dealing in detail with this literature (see Mirjana
Morokvasic's chapter in this volume) but refer to two articles,
one by Godula Kosack (1976), the other by Nermin Abadan-
Unat (1977).

In Kosack's view migration will lead to emancipation if
migrant women are 'actively involved in the production process, having the same power as productive workers and getting involved in struggles' (1976, p. 378).   She also suggests that 'it is mainly in the process of labour and political
struggle' (p. 378) that men and women realise that it is
essential to change their relationships, for example, in men
being forced to look after their children.

Abadan-Unat discusses the implications of migration on
emancipation and what she terms 'pseudo-emancipation' of
Turkish women.   She argues that migrant families abroad

become more egalitarian and women come to exert more influence in decision-making (p. 36);   she also argues in relation
to the entry into waged work that 'independent earnings,
satisfactory income and the possibility of saving are all emancipation promoting factors' (ibid., p. 39).   Abadan-Unat
uses the concept of 'pseudo-emancipation' for the women in
their native country.   The most relevant aspect of the new
freedom for these women is that they dispose independently
over money, which leads to 'conspicuous consumption'.   This
does not 'liberate' them, but serves as an escape mechanism
(ibid., p. 52).

In our view both authors lay too much emphasis on participation in the production process in analysing the overall situation of women and fail to explain convincingly how this
results in an 'egalitarian' relationship between men and
women.   In order to examine gender relations we believe
that the sexual division of labour is a more useful conceptual
starting point, because it avoids a narrow economistic bias.

The sexual division of labour is more than an allocation of
activities, it implies a power relationship between the sexes -
in which women are controlled by men - mediated by ideology.
Thus the sexual division of labour is not a natural division,
it is based on the social construction of gender identity
(Rubin, 1975, p. 178).   To examine the sexual division of
labour it is therefore not enough to look at the sex specificity
of tasks, the allocation and control of the products of labour
and the existing justifications for gender subordination must
also be taken into account (Edholm, Harris and Young, 1977,
p. 122).

In this chapter we will analyse how external migration
effects the control of men over Turkish rural women within
the spheres of gender identity, marriage and labour.   We
begin by examining control mechanisms in the Turkish context
and then go on to discuss changes in control which have
occurred as a result of migration to the Netherlands.

ARPA, THE VILLAGE

In Turkey, as in most Muslim countries, there is a strong
sexual division of labour in almost all aspects of life.   When
entering the sandy streets of Arpa it is likely that one will
first see only women: at work in the yards around the
houses, cleaning vegetables or doing washing typically squat-
ted with their heels flat on the ground.   The older women
sit in front of their houses keeping an eye on the younger
children.   Approaching the centre of Arpa you will see many
women and young girls around the tap, washing or waiting to
fill their buckets and plastic jerrycans, talking and joking.
Across the street from the tap you will finally see the men,
standing in groups, talking and smoking European tobacco.

Most of them will be either too young, too old or medically 'unfit' to be migrant workers and others will have been expelled from advanced industrial Western Europe, their labour power no longer required there.

The main economic activity of Arpa is subsistence farming, though there is some cultivation of cash crops and herding. The village is situated in the mountains of Central Turkey, a region well known for its conservatism and strict adherence to Islamic traditions. Many of the migrant workers in the Netherlands originate from this region. Arpa has approximately 1,200 inhabitants living in about 200 households, it has a small grocery store, a mosque and a primary school. Electricity had only been available in the two years prior to our visit, and there is no piped water supply which means that women must still fetch water at the tap in the centre of Arpa. A paved road connects Arpa to the nearest provincial town, approximately 30 kilometres and the only form of public transport is a minibus which makes a return trip to the town once a day.

Winters are very cold with heavy snow and summers very hot and dry, most of the rain falling in the spring. Villagers' plots are situated in a fertile valley near Arpa and are divided into small fields as a result of the inheritance system. The land is owned by the father of the family and at death his possessions including farmland, garden and vineyard are divided amongst his children. Under Turkish law daughters and sons inherit equally, but in practice only the division of farmland is carried out in accordance with this law. In the division of the garden and the vineyard the traditional Islamic law is followed resulting in sons inheriting twice as much as daughters.

GENDER IDENTITY

In order to analyse the mechanisms which control all aspects of Turkish women's lives we need to outline briefly the ideas which surround the conception of 'femininity' prevalent in Turkish society. Notions of what constitutes femininity and masculinity are very pronounced with the relationship between the genders being a hierarchical one, implying that female qualities are of lower value.

While our observations are limited to Arpa we have good reason to believe that they can be generalised to rural Turkish society as a whole. Arpa villagers speak of women in four categories: 'çocuk' (child), 'gelinlik' (marriageable girl), 'gelin' (married women), and 'ihtiyar' (old person). The categorisation corresponds to the female cycle of sexual development. (4) An additional set of terms makes a distinction between females who are untouched, known as girl ('kiz'), while the term woman ('kadin') denotes those who have had

sexual intercourse. The term 'kiz' corresponds rigidly to
the first stages in a female's life cycle and the term 'kadin'
corresponds to the remaining two. The classifications illustrate the force of the sexual division of labour which allocates
to women no other socially acceptable role than becoming a
wife and a mother. (5)

During our stay in Arpa we did not meet any women older
than twenty-five years of age who were still unmarried. On
the contrary, it is common for girls to get married between
fourteen and nineteen years of age. (6)

Whether we think of a girl in her childhood or of a married
woman, women are always subject to male guardianship. Explanations put forward by villagers can be summarised as
follows: 'This is necessary because women happen to be weak
and men happen to be aggressive. That's the way they are
created.' Islam serves to justify the existing sexual division
of labour with women confronted by divine rules regulating
their behaviour. But because women are not allowed in the
mosques (except during the fasting month of Ramadan) their
knowledge of the Koran is mediated by men. Nevertheless
Arpa women tend to observe Islamic practice more than Arpa
men (see also Maher, 1981, p. 82).

In her study of male and female dynamics in Morocco,
Mernissi analyses the relationship between Islam and the position of women. She identifies in Islam the idea that women
are powerful and dangerous beings, symbols of disorder, and
the fear that a growing relationship between men and women
would threaten the devotion a man should have for Allah.
To avoid this, the intimacy between men and women is limited
to sexual intimacy (Mernissi, 1975, p. viii). This is why
this sphere is crucial to the manifestation of male dominance,
with the sexuality of women controlled by men.

Thus when a girl becomes marriageable in rural Turkey the
exercise of control by men in her family concentrates on her
virginity. The notion of virginity is a broad one, even
speaking to a man can damage virginity, so the latter implies
the observance of modest behaviour, including avoidance of
contact with men. When a girl is married this control is
transferred to her family by marriage and serves to protect
the monopoly a husband has over his wife. It is important
to realise that - though protection of the family honour has to
do with male prestige - not only men exercise control over
women. Elder women in particular have internalised the
values and norms legitimating control of women.

Control takes place through restrictions on women's activities and their freedom of movement. In the latter case our
observations in Arpa indicated that these restrictions were not
as rigidly applied in the village and its environs as they were
in the provincial town nearby. For instance in Arpa marriageable girls went alone every summer morning into the
mountains to mind goats and married women frequently visited
relatives or neighbours during the evening.

Nevertheless male and female spheres are clearly demarca-
ted. The separation of the sexes is directed at reducing
the possibility of women being sexually 'defiled', which would
lead to the loss of 'male honour' within the family.

MARRIAGE

Marriages in Arpa are highly endogamous, many being arranged between first cousins. Family members play a major
role in the arrangement of marriages and while fathers under-
take the role of negotiator, female relatives from the prospective husband's family also exert some influence. The latter
are said to be the best advisers because they are acquainted
with the girls and also the qualities a good wife should
possess.
Traditionally the views of the couple were not taken into
consideration, it was strictly a matter between parents, particularly fathers. Nowadays girls are often approached first
by a messenger of the boy which gives her a chance to
refuse before there is any parental intervention. Sometimes
a couple can reach an agreement in this way which their
parents refuse to consider, Nuran explained her own case:
'Hasan and I had seen each other during milking-time in the
mountains. I liked him and apparently he liked me,
because his father came one evening to see my parents.
They did not agree, however, because he comes from a
poor family. When we would not change their minds we
decided to flee to the mountains where we spent the night.
Of course everyone found out soon enough. My parents
could not but accept the marriage, since I was no longer a
virgin. Still, it hurts because I am not allowed to talk to
them anymore.'
Nuran's story illustrates the consequences of such behaviour:
she has disgraced her parents who refuse to talk to her.
In these circumstances only her father can re-establish contact with her. In Arpa elopements are not exceptional (7)
and should be distinguished from bride-capture. The latter
involves a forced marriage without the girl's consent and is
considered a very serious crime in Turkey, punishable by
long prison sentences. In Arpa only one case of bride-
capture was mentioned to us. (8)
After a marriage has been agreed upon by both families,
goods are exchanged. The most important exchange is the
giving of golden jewellery to the bride by the groom, (9)
gifts of jewellery increasingly replace the gift of land. This
change marks the penetration of the cash economy into the
village, a development which migration has stimulated. The
gift of jewellery becomes the bride's property unless she herself sues for divorce. Although this property is seen as a
security fund in case of repudiation, women often sell their

jewellery if it is seen to be in the family interest, for example, to finance migration to Western Europe.

The actual wedding involves the whole village. A major event is the carrying off on horseback of the bride by the husband's male relatives, though cars are beginning to replace horses. The bride is carried to her husband's parental home and the wedding night establishes for the groom whether or not his wife is a virgin. If the husband says she is not, the girl is sent back to her parents (see Anthias, also in this volume). In the case of one woman in Arpa, Semra, the groom claimed she was not 'untouched' (10) and because as a woman she did not have the right to defend herself, he sent her away and demanded that his jewellery should be returned. Semra is now married to a widower and raises his three children.

Marriages in Arpa are nowadays normally registered in the nearby town although the Islamic consecration is considered of primary importance. Registration is rarely practised however in the case of divorce. (11) Arpa has a long tradition of a high divorce rate which has not dramatically changed since migration began. Nearly all divorces are repudiations and subsequent marriages are only consecrated by the 'hoca' (local religious leader) so they are not registered. (12)

An accepted reason for a husband to repudiate his wife is 'female infertility'. Having children is a prerequisite for a successful marriage, being a 'good wife' includes providing the family with children. If women cannot fulfil this task which is allocated to them according to the sexual division of labour they are deemed to have failed in their role as a wife.

Migration adds a new dimension to repudiations and divorces. Many women left behind are suddenly confronted with the news that they have been set aside in favour of a European or Turkish woman living in Western Europe. In these circumstances women can and do successfully refuse an official divorce. The case of Kesban illustrates this point: her husband had been working in Europe for several years and was having an affair with a European woman whom he wanted to marry in order to get a residence permit. He returned to Arpa to divorce Kesban but she refused and he acquiesced.

In the case of a divorce or repudiation children usually stay with their father and the mother loses her children. However great the pain of parting with her children the woman will normally do so because it is not socially acceptable for her to remain single and children will lessen her chances of remarrying. At the same time men are reluctant to care for the children of their previous marriage.

The automatic allotment of children to husbands obviously consolidates existing power relations. At the same time it individualises women, because they have to pass their children on.

LABOUR

The division of domestic and agricultural labour is assigned according to sex, which in theory means women must perform domestic tasks and men agricultural work. In practice women perform all domestic tasks which include the cultivation of crops for household consumption and the caring of animals. They also perform agricultural tasks at harvest time.

The sex-hierarchisation of tasks in Arpa is quite clear, with women's labour deemed of lesser value than men's. But there is also a hierarchy of women's tasks according to the female cycle of sexual development, girls and daughters-in-law having to perform work with the lowest value, while mothers-in-law are relieved of the burden of housework.

On a daily basis women take care of the household and the family. They bake bread and cook meals. As visitors we were expected on several occasions to eat with the male members of the household while the wife and daughters sat in the kitchen. Only when we had finished our meal did they start to eat in the kitchen. Women also wash dishes, clean the house and fetch water, but these are all tasks in which they are often helped by their daughters.

Child care is normally shared among female kin, but a mother will carry her child on her back until it is two or three years of age while she goes about her work. When the child can walk well the responsibility of child care is shared by all women and girls in the family.

Another labour intensive task is the washing of clothes. Water must be fetched from the tap in the middle of the village and then boiled before washing can begin. During the winter women weave carpets and make clothes. Some women have a sewing machine with which they make the clothes for their own family, and sometimes for other families for which they are paid. This extra source of money can be an important contribution to the income of women whose husbands have migrated but have not yet sent remittances.

In addition to the farmland every household owns a garden (sometimes located at a considerable distance from the village) where crops are cultivated for household consumption. Apart from ploughing, the garden is mainly cultivated by women and girls. The cultivated crops include beans, corn, onions, tomatoes, peppers, cucumbers and potatoes. Women and girls go to their gardens virtually every day and it can take an hour's donkey ride to get there. Mothers teach their daughters how to cultivate the land and at the age of twelve daughters are allowed to go alone to the garden.

Women must also take care of the cattle and milk them. Every household has some cows which are milked early in the morning and after milking they are rounded up with the donkeys and taken into the mountains to graze until evening. In the summer months sheep and goats graze far from the

village in the mountains and girls are expected to get up
very early to go and milk them there.   The milk is proces-
sed by the women into cheese, butter and yoghurt.

According to the sexual division of labour the agricultural
tasks of ploughing and sowing is men's work.   The most
important crops are rye, wheat, barley, Spanish beans and
sunflowers.   Harvest begins in June and is the busiest time
of the year for everyone, with men, women and children all
participating.   Daughters-in-law are required to help their
husband's family and migrant women, home on holiday, are
expected to work as hard at harvest time as everyone else.

The migration of so many men from the village has had a
dramatic effect on agriculture.   Because of the rigidity of
the sexual division of labour women cannot take over the
tasks allocated to men in the agricultural sphere.   It is
argued that women cannot use a plough because it is too
heavy for them, thus a substantial part of the land is no
longer cultivated.

After harvest the women clean and process the crops in
preparation for storage and use in the winter.   The processing of the yearly grape harvest is an additional task.   Har-
vesting grapes is the only task that women took over from
men when migration started.   Women are said not to be able
to use machines and machinery is not used in grape harvest-
ing.   Women dry the juiceless grapes in the sun until they
become raisins, but men continue to have responsibility for
their sale in the nearby town.   We met some older women
who undertook such transactions themselves because their
husbands were in Western Europe and they had no father-in-
law or brother who could take over the task.   The juicy
grapes are used to make a grape syrup, 'pekmez'.   Before
migration men undertook the task of extracting the juice by
treading them in a big stone well.   Nowadays women under-
take this task, so that in this sphere the sexual division of
labour is no longer rigidly applied.

MIGRATION: THE WOMEN-LEFT-BEHIND

About twenty years ago the first men left Arpa to migrate to
Western Europe, leaving their wives behind.   Since 1975 and
the easing of restrictions on family re-union, a number of
women have left the village to join their husbands, but the
majority of women stay behind or come back before their husband's return.   Men usually visit their wives once a year,
but in the case of illegal migrants it might take several years
before they return.   In the meantime such men keep in touch
with their wives through messages conducted by other visiting
villagers.

All the women we met who were left in Arpa expressed a
desire to join their husbands in Western Europe.   Explana-

tions included the anticipation of a lightening of their work load and the fear of divorce. But men often object to family reunion, arguing that it is too expensive and bad for the morality of women and children. (13)

In her description of the effects of migration on the women left behind in Turkey, Abadan-Unat suggests that migration does not affect the fertility rate in rural areas. She suggests that women solve the loneliness and separation from their husbands by having children with great frequency, 'To be pregnant or having breast fed infants keeps a woman emotionally satisfied' (1977, p. 48). We cannot wholly endorse such a conclusion from our experiences in Arpa. When we talked to Pervin about contraception in Western Europe she angrily demanded;

'Why did you not bring these pills with you? I am expecting my seventh children. My husband works abroad for twelve years and I have to raise the children without men. My husband comes only two months a year and my father-in-law is dead.'

Abadan-Unat also suggests that women are free to decide whether they have children or not. In Arpa women's control of their own fertility is far from self-evident. There is little knowledge of modern contraceptive methods which cannot in any case be purchased in the village. A woman would have to go to town and have access to the money necessary to purchase a contraceptive device.

Birth control largely takes place through the practice of coitus interruptus, the few women who do use modern contraceptive methods are usually those who have lived in Western Europe for a period of years. The primary schoolteacher in Arpa acts as a confidant to women who come to her for advice on matters of sexuality.

With respect to decision-making and authority Abadan-Unat describes the 'pseudo-emancipation' of the women left behind induced by migration; 'Women have become the major persons to whom cash income is sent by mail or bank service' (ibid., 1977, p. 52). The term 'pseudo-emancipation' is used to describe the ability of women to spend remittance money themselves. Abadan-Unat also suggests that living in a nuclear family means more authority for women left behind who are now head of the household (ibid., p. 49; see also Kiray, 1976). When we consider the position of women left behind in the migration process in Arpa we find that, although there are many nuclear households, this has had little effect on the pattern of decision-making or the authority of women.

Whether or not they live in an independent household, the mother-in-law continues to exercise some control over her daughter-in-law's labour. The women always work with their parents-in-law in the garden and on the land during harvest time. Usually it is their father-in-law who represents the husband in selling agricultural produce, in buying wood, coal,

etc., for the winter.   And it is usually the father-in-law
who receives remittances from Western Europe.   Only when
the father-in-law is very old or has died are women allowed
to handle such transactions themselves.   Even then some
women cannot take over these responsibilities because male
guardianship passes to her husband's male relatives.   Nevertheless there are indications that this is changing.   More
recently some women in Arpa have gone to the nearby town
to collect remittance money themselves.   This trend will
probably continue and extend in future as it has done elsewhere in Turkey (see Kiray, 1976).   Aliye is exceptional,
she does manage her own livelihood and income:
   'My husband works in the Netherlands for almost ten years
   now.   My three children and myself live from the sale of
   the agricultural produce, which I sell myself in town.   I
   don't need my husband's money, I can take care of myself.'
Aliye demonstrates pride in her labour but she also controls
the product of that labour and has her own source of income.
Women generally demonstrate pride in their labour and their
contribution is recognised by men;   nevertheless women generally derive no power from this because they do not control
the product of their labour.
   We have already mentioned the fear expressed by women
remaining in Arpa that their husbands will divorce or repudiate them in favour of a European woman.   This possibility
is often avoided because a type of polygyny has developed
along with migration. (14)   A number of husbands abroad
have found a second 'wife' in Western Europe.   The European
women may provide good accommodation, free board and lodg-
ing and a regular sexual relationship. (15)   The wife in
Arpa is usually aware· of the existence of this second 'wife'
but she is more or less forced to accept the situation because
of the far-reaching consequences that divorce would have for
her.
   The European women do not visit Arpa and the women there
assured us that they would not allow these women to enter
the village.   At the same time there have been Arpa women
who have stayed for a period in Western Europe where they
were forced to share the house with their husband's European
'wife'.

LIFE IN THE NETHERLANDS

Our fieldwork in Turkey provided us with the background
information necessary to gain a better understanding of the
changes in the position of women brought about through
migration to the Netherlands.   Changes which have an important bearing on that position include increased control of the
husband over his wife as they are forced into a direct relationship with each other and women's transition to waged

labour.   These changes mark a new objective position for
Arpa women in legal and economic relations, changes which we
believe are shared by all Mediterranean migrant women in
Western Europe.   Thus we will begin by making some general
comments about the position of migrant women in the Netherlands and then go on to specific comments about women from
Arpa.

The beginning of the 1970s marked the onset of economic
contraction in the Netherlands and rising unemployment.   In
common with all other labour importing countries in Western
Europe, the Dutch government declared a ban on the recruitment of new migrant labour.   But consistent with trends
elsewhere the number of migrants continued to rise due to the
increase in family re-unions.   As a result the composition of
the foreign population changed dramatically with the proportion of women rapidly increasing.   In 1968 there were only
412 Turkish women in the Netherlands, twelve years later
there were 44,000 (Central Bureau of Statistics, 1981).

In order to gain permission for family re-union, a male
migrant must have a regular job which he has held down for
twelve months.   He must also demonstrate to the authorities
that he can provide adequate accommodation for a family.
Meeting the housing requirement can be extremely difficult if
one appreciates the drastic shortage of housing in the Netherlands.   Apart from a relatively large number of unmarried
Yugoslavian women, few migrant women came independently to
the Netherlands.

Women who come to Holland to join their husbands legally
receive a permit conditional on residence with their husbands.
This legal position forces a woman into total dependence on
her husband.   If either partner repudiates the other or sues
for divorce within three years the woman will lose her right
to stay and has to leave the Netherlands.   Only women who
have stayed for three years without interruption in Holland
are allowed to ask for a residence permit in their own right
and they can only seek a residence permit without restrictions
if they possess a labour permit.   Both women's and migrant
organisations have protested for years against this discrimination and have made efforts to support migrant women who
have fallen victim to the ruling.   The obstacles in the path
of getting a labour permit are very great, particularly in a
period of economic contraction and rising unemployment.

GENDER IDENTITY AND MARRIAGE

Arpa migrants in Amsterdam generally live in nuclear families, (16) and while there are also nuclear families in Arpa the
separation of the sexes in daily life is not as rigid in Amsterdam as it was in Arpa.   There the mother-in-law acted as
representative of male authority and power and it was through

her that men were able to wield power over women in a situation of total separation of the sexes. In Amsterdam the
traditional pattern of the sexual division of labour is distur-
bed: husband and wife are forced into a direct relationship
with each other, a change which frequently acts as a source
of conflict between them. (17)

Arpa migrants are residentially concentrated in the nineteenth-century districts of Amsterdam. Residential concentration means close contact with other villagers and while
many women are fortunate in having relatives living in
Amsterdam some have no kin to provide emotional support.
For example Pakise explained to us:

'All my relatives live in Turkey. Sometimes I long for
them so much I have to cry. Of course there are many
people from Arpa here but they are not the same as your
family.'

The sociability and support provided by other villagers and
people from the same region is particularly important for Arpa
women and usually provides the only possibility they have of
meeting people. This is partly due to the husband's fear of
contamination by the 'European dissolute way of life' which
offends his entire value system and often results in a severe
over protection of women to prevent the undermining of this
value system. Compared to life in Arpa it means in practice
a reduced freedom of movement for women which in turn
diminishes the possibility of Turkish women orientating themselves to Dutch society. (18) The situation is further com-
plicated by language problems, cultural difference and discrimination, all of which result in a tendency to remain within
the 'known' social world of the Turkish community and the
avoidance of contact with the Dutch as much as possible.

As we have suggested the large concentration of Arpa villagers has advantages for women but the disadvantages are
equally apparent, it also fosters the conditions which support
the control of other villagers, men and women, over the
observance of traditional norms of behaviour. One girl explained to us:

'After much discussion with my parents they accepted that
I did not have to wear scarves anymore. But one day on
my way to market, I passed some men from Arpa in the
street. I saw them looking at me and thinking, bad girl.
The news spread rapidly, gossip started and letters came
from Turkey. And although my parents did not force me
I finally gave in and started to wear scarves again.'

There are instances where women are forced to return to
Arpa under pressure of gossip, if they do not go their husbands will lose their good name. Frequently women have to
return to care for ageing parents-in-law, which indicates the
persistence of traditional values regarding obligations within
the extended family.

Earlier we spoke of the practice of bride-capture in Turkey.

Recently a number of cases have occurred in the Netherlands, the girls in question being the daughters of Turkish migrants with legal residence permits.   Illegal migrants could legalise their position through marriage to these girls whom they captured and raped in an attempt to force marriage.   In other cases large sums of money, or golden jewellery have been paid by illegal migrants to marry legally resident girls creating a situation where the latter become 'valuable commodities' in the Netherlands.

Finally there is the question of the control of women's fertility.   Arpa women in Amsterdam usually know about modern contraception and practise it.   Nevertheless some women fear that their fertility will be damaged in the process.   To reiterate according to the sexual division of labour a woman must provide the family with children and failure to do so may lead to repudiation or divorce.   Men take the view that it is the woman's responsibility to take charge of an effective contraceptive method.   On the other hand they retain control over fertility in deciding when contraception should stop even though this is often sooner than the wife desires.

LABOUR

As a result of migration the content of domestic labour has changed.   In rural Turkey we have seen that domestic labour is not confined to 'housework'.   It includes labouring in the garden and caring for animals.   In industrialised Holland women perform domestic tasks within the isolation of the nuclear family.   Much of the skilled work performed by women within the domestic sphere in Turkey becomes obsolete in the Netherlands.   Although it was hard work we have noted that women express a strong pride in their labour. Having said this all women see 'housework' in the Netherlands as having certain advantages, as Hacer explained:

'Housework in Holland is so easy and it takes less time than in Turkey.   I do not have to walk anymore to fetch water and I can buy say tomatoes in the supermarket without having to grow them myself.   For washing and cleaning I use machines.'

But child care is a very different matter.   In Arpa there is always somebody in the neighbourhood who will keep an eye on the children.   In Amsterdam the nuclear family structure means the disappearance of shared child care.   Substitutes in the form of state or private provision are both scarce and expensive and in these circumstances if there is an elder daughter present her secondary education may suffer or be dispensed with in order that she can look after her younger brothers and sisters while parents work.   Some Arpa women hand over their children to other Arpa women, for the day.

Family re-union is an expensive business.   An urban
family divorced from the land requires a large amount of cash
to get by.   But migrants have additional financial obligations
in the form of remittances to support relatives remaining in
Turkey and also the maintenance of return visits.   Furthermore most migrants are 'target' workers, saving for some
future return and often paying instalments on a house in the
homeland.   One income is usually inadequate to meet all
these commitments and while a man may seek an extra job in
many cases wives also seek waged work.   According to
Islamic tradition men are the sole providers of a family income
but migration has forced a departure from this norm.   As
Gül, a very religious woman, told us;
  'In the beginning I found it very hard to go out to work.
  But now, that I am almost forty it is not so difficult anymore.   It is not so bad for older women to go out to
  work.'
According to official figures Turkish and Yugoslavian women
have the highest rates of labour force participation amongst
Mediterranean women in the Netherlands.   But these official
figures are not an accurate record due to the number of
Turkish women working illegally both inside and outside the
home in the absence of a work permit.   Nevertheless official
figures indicate that Turkish women are concentrated in unskilled manual work in laundries, cleaning and as production
workers in the clothing, textiles and food industries.   Their
working conditions are often unsatisfactory involving dangerous work with inadequate safety precautions.
Turkish women occupy a very vulnerable position in the
Dutch labour market resulting in a high level of exploitation.
Sirin, an Arpa woman, recounted the following story:
  'I had done some overtime during the week-end but at the
  end of the week I did not receive the extra money for it.
  I have worked for a couple of years, I know my rights and
  speak enough Dutch to express myself.   As soon as I
  complained to the boss he said it must have been a mistake
  and finally I got my money.'
Sirin is in a better position than the majority of the Turkish
migrant women whose command of Dutch is very poor.
In common with every other country in advanced industrial
Western Europe the clothing industry in the Netherlands has
become a niche for migrant women workers.   Low paid piece-
work is a key factor in the economic viability of the small
inner-city sweatshops, yet these wages are indispensable to
migrant women who pass work on to each other.
The clothing sweatshops also provide Turkish women who
stay at home with the possibility of earning money.   There
is no official record of how many Turkish or other migrant
women are occupied as homeworkers but it is possibly quite
high.   For migrant women with small children or husbands
who forbid their wives to leave the home on their own, home-

working is a necessity. Child-care responsibilities also force many women into part-time work at unsocial hours. Many of the women from Arpa worked as cleaners either early in the morning or in the evenings or whenever they could arrange child care with their eldest daughter or with their husband.

Participation in the labour market can improve migrant women's legal position in Dutch society if they obtain legal work. But access to a wage does not necessarily imply control over the spending of that wage. The majority of Arpa women give their money to their husbands without apparent conflict, as far as we know. However disputes over control of the wage are cited as the major source of conflict by Turkish women seeking shelter in the refuges for battered women in Amsterdam, and Abadan-Unat also suggests that family finance organisation is a major source of conflict amongst Turkish couples (1977, p. 41).

CONCLUSION

In this paper we have chosen not to follow Kosack and Abadan-Unat in evaluating the effects of migration primarily in terms of emancipation. We have chosen to examine the effects of migration on the position of women through an analysis of differing control mechanisms of men over women in a number of different spheres.

In Arpa the sexual division of labour results in a separate women's sphere indirectly controlled by men in which women have a certain freedom of movement and autonomy. The maintenance of this separate women's sphere in the Netherlands leads to an increase in male control over women's freedom of movement, not a reduction in control.

Arpa women are glad to be relieved of the control exercised by the mother-in-law and other relatives by marriage. But settling as a nuclear family does not always live up to these expectations as the traditional power of the mother-in-law is transferred to the husband. In discussing the isolation of Arpa women in Amsterdam it is important to distinguish between their relations within the Turkish community and Dutch society. Arpa women in Amsterdam have intensive social contact with each other. These contacts act as an important source of support in an otherwise strange and sometimes hostile world, but also as a source of social control over women. With respect to Dutch society, Arpa women are truly isolated.

Finally in Arpa women derive a certain autonomy and self-esteem from their labour which is largely denied to them in the migration setting. In Holland they are confined to low status and low paid work, thus we disagree with Kosack who argues that participation in the production process as wage labourers will lead to emancipation. Involvement in waged labour does not in itself lead to emancipation, particularly if a woman does not even control the spending of her wage. Any evaluation of the effects of the transition to waged labour amongst migrant women must take into account the intricate system of power relations and control mechanisms which operate within the family.

NOTES

1 The research was carried out between February 1980 and January 1981, resulting in a master's thesis, under the supervision of An Huitzing at the University of Amsterdam. Thanks are due to Anna Aaiten, Britt Fontaine, Marijke Mossink, Saskia Wieringa, Marion den Uyl and Annie Phizacklea for their useful comments on a draft version of the paper.

2 According to official figures there were 247,000 migrants from the Mediterranean countries in Holland (1 January 1980). The Turkish constitute the largest subgroup, 106,700, of which 44,000 are women and 62,700 men (Central Bureau of Statistics). In Amsterdam out of a total of 40,170 Mediterranean migrants, there are 12,384 Turkish migrants, of which 5,355 are females and 7,029 male (Bureau of Statistics of Amsterdam, 1 January 1980).

3 To protect the identity of those mentioned in this study, we have changed the names of persons and the village. We would like to thank the people of Arpa for their hospitality and assistance.

4 Engelbrektsson found the same classification (1978, p. 134). She studied the emigration process of two Turkish villages, whose inhabitants went to Sweden. Both villages are in the same district as Arpa.

5 Rubin suggests that heterosexuality as a predominant norm is fundamental to the sex-gender system (1975, p. 180).

6 In the past girls used to marry somewhere around their first menstruation, because this made them 'gelinlik' (marriageable). Nowadays there is a rise in the age of marriage.

7 Elopements are also mentioned by Engelbrektsson (1978, p. 149). She describes it as the only way of escape for young people, which is accepted as such by the non-involved.

8 Engelbrektsson also found that bride-capture only occurred rarely (1978, p. 150).

9 The value of the jewellery can be as much as 2,000 English pounds, though we also heard of an amount of 10,000 English pounds in the case of a migrant girl. Heavy inflation of Turkish currency however makes it difficult to give exact amounts.

10   We never ascertained as to whether girls used substitutes, such as chicken's blood, if they were not sure
their hymen was undamaged (whether by 'innocent' causes
as donkey-riding, or by premarital sexual intercourse).

11   Ataturks' reforms during his reign as the first president
of the Turkish republic included the legal right for women
to get a divorce.   In the case of an official divorce,
both parties have to agree.   So if women do not want it,
they can stop it.

12   When repudiations are prevalent, as we see in Arpa, it is
nearly impossible to compare the divorce rate with other
places in Turkey, because repudiations are not registered.   Therefore divorce statistics in Turkey are
underestimates.

13   Engelbrektsson found the same reasoning of migrant husbands and their wives left behind (1978, p. 130).

14   In Turkey polygamy is officially forbidden, since Ataturks
introduced his reforms.

15   The same thing happened in the case of the men who
went to Sweden, described by Engelbrektsson (1978, p.
273).

16   The family is sometimes extended by male relatives
belonging to the man's or woman's family.   These relatives may be illegally working, unmarried young men or
legally working married men, who left their wives behind.

17   In spite of this, divorces asked for by Arpa women still
have not occurred, though Turkish women in general ask
for divorce more and more.

18   The same fear causes girls to be kept at home after they
have finished primary school.   Parents are afraid that -
due to mixed classes at school - their daughters' behaviour would fall below their expectations, implying disgrace
for the family and losing her chances of a good marriage.
We should add that sometimes this reasoning is misused by
parents who need their daughters' help at home in order
for both to be able to work, or they keep her from school
and send her to work in a factory instead.

7 Transnational production and women workers

Mary Hancock

INTRODUCTION

Over the last ten to fifteen years extensive changes have
occurred in the world economy with the rapid development
and expansion of transnational production. Transnational
corporations have established global patterns of production
and labour under which high-technology, capital-intensive
production is carried out in the highly industrialised countries of Western Europe, USA and Japan, while the low-technology, labour-intensive production is occurring increasingly
in 'off-shore' sites in less-developed, Third World countries,
involving a predominantly female workforce.

One of the key issues therefore that needs to be explored
is why this phenomena has evolved. The material presented
in this study indicates that this global network of transnational production (found particularly in the electronics,
textiles, clothing and food industries) has developed as transnational corporations have moved their assembly production
offshore to sites in South-East Asia, Central and South
America, Eire and Portugal in search of low-wage labour, in
order to maximise their profits. In this process the target
group is women who are being primarily sought as cheap
labour and consequently the assembly workforce that is being
employed in this labour-intensive stage of production in the
offshore sites is largely comprised of young female workers,
many of whom have recently migrated from rural to urban
areas for such 'first time' employment.

The targeting of women as a cheap labour force has thus
been a key factor in the development of transnational production with its movement offshore. However, much of the current literature available on these issues has failed to discuss
or analyse this widespread exploitation of female labour - and
in so doing has once again rendered women invisible. The
following study is part of the process that is beginning to
redress the conspiracy of silence and as such it will examine
the issue of transnational production and the exploitation of
women workers through a case study of the United States
electronics industry in South-East Asia and the Pacific - an
industry heavily dependent on a low-wage, predominantly
migrant, female workforce.

The material drawn on for this study comes primarily from
the preliminary findings of a project established in 1978 to

examine the impact of transnational corporations on women workers in Asia and the Pacific. This cross-cultural research project was co-ordinated by the Culture Learning Institute of the East West Center in Honolulu, Hawaii and involved a study of transnational corporations in the First World, e.g., USA and Japan, and their impact on Third World countries, e.g. in South-East Asia, and peripheral nations such as New Zealand. (1)

THE INTERNATIONAL DIVISION OF PRODUCTION

Since the mid-sixties the electronics industry (which involves the production and marketing of electronic components and products such as consumer, industrial and military goods) has expanded to a global level through a system in which companies in the process of manufacturing an electronic component or product carry out their different levels of production in sites in various nations.

With the US electronics industry this transnational production process generally consists of several integrated steps. The first step involves high-technology production in America which is capital intensive and heavily reliant on a professional and technical workforce, who carry out development, design, engineering and testing of the product. In the second stage, labour-intensive, low-technology final assembly production and testing of the product is carried out - frequently in offshore plants in South-East Asia. The goods which have been sent to the offshore plant for final assembly are then exported back to the home country base (USA) for sales and marketing. This international division of production which is closely integrated between the home country and offshore site is vividly illustrated through an analysis of the nature of the work undertaken in each area, for example in the USA, in the Santa Clara Valley, near San Francisco which is the key electronics production base for companies in the USA; the major job categories in the industry are shown in Table 7.1

TABLE 7.1 *Major employment categories for Santa Clara electronics workforce*

Category	Per cent of total electronics workforce
Manager	13.2
Professional	25.6
Sales	1.3
Clerical	15.1
Production	44.8

Source: Axelrad and PHASE staff, 1979, p. 22. (2)

The professional and non-factory-floor production sectors account for 55.2 per cent of the industry and for the total US electronics semi-conductor industry in 1977 product workers account for only 55 per cent of the workforce (US Department of Commerce, 1979 quoted in Snow, 1980). Thus professional and technical work play a very significant role in the US factories and in the industry generally.

In the offshore factories of US companies in South-East Asia there is a completely different situation, in which assembly production accounts for 85 per cent to 90 per cent of the work, as illustrated by the example of a Singapore industry survey in 1977, the findings of which are in Table 7.2.

TABLE 7.2 *Singapore workforce categories 1977*

Category	Per cent of workforce
Technicians	5
White-collar workers	5
Supervisors	3
Production operatives	87

Source: 'Business Times', Singapore, 21 November 1977.

Thus as L.Y.C. Lim found in her extensive study of the electronics industry in Malaysia and Singapore, 'Today well over 90% of all assembly operatives of U.S. electronics firms are conducted overseas...' (Lim, 1978, p. 5).

This highly integrated system of transnational production in the electronics industry with the international division of production between the highly industrialised US and developing Third World countries began with early moves towards offshore production in the 1960s by US corporations into South-East Asia. The first plant was established in Hong Kong (1961) and offshore production gradually emerged in other South-East Asian countries including South Korea (1964), Taiwan (1964), Singapore (1967), Malaysia (1972), Indonesia (1972) and then more recently in the Philippines (1974) and Thailand (1974). (3) Since the first tentative moves offshore there has been a proliferation in the number of US assembly plants in South-East Asia. For example, the North American Congress on Latin America (NACLA) reported that, in 1976, 194 US electronics offshore assembly plants were operating in South-East Asia. (4) Many of the US corporations have developed multiplant operations, with offshore assembly work in more than one country. For example Fairchild Camera and Instruments Corporation and National Semiconductor Corporation both have six different offshore assembly plants in South-East Asia while General Electric Company and Motorola

Incorporated both operate four such plants (Snow, 1979).
It is suggested that operating with a variety of offshore
plants in a range of countries ensures that companies maximise on the availability of labour and low wages and enables
production to be ongoing in cases of political, social or labour
instability in one country.   On the basis of a sample of fifteen of the major US corporations, UNCTAD have compiled
statistics which illustrate the development and growth of US
electronics offshore operations in South-East Asia (1975).
The data show that a variety of US electronics firms operate
in a range of South-East Asian countries, and their number
of employees has rapidly expanded from 15,000 in 1971 to
over 50,000 in 1974.   The electronic component products that
are being assembled include capacitors, resistors and semi-
conductors.

THE INTERNATIONAL SEXUAL DIVISION OF LABOUR

The transnational electronics industry with its international
division of production between the industrialised and Third
World nations has also created, and is dependent upon, an
international sexual division of labour.   In the US men play
a predominant role in the high-technology areas of the industry, while women are largely located in semi-skilled, low-
technology assembly production. (5)   This pattern is shown
in Table 7.3.

TABLE 7.3 *Sexual division of labour in Santa Clara Valley,
California, electronic workforce*

Job category	Per cent job category filled by women	Per cent job category filled by men
Professional	10.7	89.3
Manager	8.4	91.6
Sales	12.1	87.9
Clerical	84.1	15.9
Technician	19.4	80.6
Craft	23.9	76.1
Assembly	76.4	23.6
Labourer	78.9	21.1
Service/ maintenance	8.5	91.5

Source: Axelrad, 1979, p. 23.

From Table 7.3 one can see how, in the Santa Clara electronics workforce in the US, men occupy the technical (80.6
per cent), professional (89.3 per cent), managerial (91.6 per
cent) and craft (76.1 per cent) positions.   In contrast,
women are mainly employed in clerical (84.1 per cent), labour
(78.9 per cent) and assembly (76.4 per cent).   Thus
although in 1978, 52 per cent of all US electronics employees
were women - they were largely found in production work
(US Department of Labor, 1979 quoted in Snow, 1980, p.
13).   For example, the US Equal Employment Opportunity
Commission reported that 89.7 per cent of all women in the
US electronics industry were in three occupational categories.
57.8 per cent were operatives, 13.1 per cent were labourers
and 18.8 per cent were office and clerical workers (1975, p.
103).
    In the US offshore sites in South-East Asia the sexual divi-
sion of labour is extreme.   In the electronics plants of the
Philippines, Malaysia, Singapore and Thailand over 90 per
cent of the workforce is female (Lim, 1978;   Blake and Moonstan, 1980;   Sanchez, 1978).   But not only are women almost
all the employees in these US offshore sites, they are also
predominantly low-technology, semi-skilled assembly workers
(for South-East Asia, see Grossman, 1979 and Lim, 1978;   for
Mexico, see Ladman, 1977).   Thus transnational production
in the electronics industry has developed a global division of
labour which is made up of a high-technology, predominantly
male professional and technical workforce in the US, supported by a labour-intensive, semi-skilled, assembly production
workforce almost completely comprised of women workers from
the US and to a greater extent women workers from offshore
sites in South-East Asia. (6)

LOW-WAGE FEMALE LABOUR

The key factor behind this development has been the constant
search by company management in an industry which is
highly competitive and labour intensive for ways of cutting
costs, and maintaining and increasing profits.   Thus the
payment of low wages to an offshore assembly workforce and
the employment of a low-wage female workforce in the industry
generally has been a major strategy that has enabled the industry to grow and profit at a phenomenal rate: 'It has
been estimated that the electronics industry is growing 50%
faster than the rest of industry and the semiconductor industry 50% faster than electronics' (Heikes, quoted in Sciberras,
1977, p. 48).   In 1969 wages in offshore plants were generally at least ten times lower than those paid in the US (US
Tariff Commission, 1970).   In 1978 in the US Bay Area electronics industry sector, an electronics assembly worker received an average salary from between $4.37 to $5.58 per

hour (American Electronics Association, 1978 quoted in
Axelrad, 1979, p. 25).   This wage is still a great deal
higher than an assembly worker received in a US offshore
plant, where in 1976 wages ranged from 17 cents to 62 cents
per hour as shown in Table 7.4   While employing a large
assembly workforce in offshore plants in South-East Asia on
much lower wages than are paid in the US for comparable
work – the employment of a (low wage) female workforce
throughout the industry in both the US and offshore plants
also ensures lower production costs and greater profits for
the companies.

TABLE 7.4 *Assembly worker average hourly wages (US $) in
US offshore plants (1976)*

Country	Hourly wage*
Indonesia	.17
Thailand	.26
Philippines	.32
India	.37
Taiwan	.37
Malaysia	.41
South Korea	.52
Hong Kong	.55
Singapore	.62

* Calculated as an average between monthly high and low
  wage rates for a standard 46-hour week.

Source: 'Business Asia', 30 April 1976, quoted in NACLA,
1977, p. 15.

Table 7.5 gives examples of the low wages received by
women workers in offshore plants set against a calculation of
the monthly expenses or basic cost for one person for rent,
food and transportation in four South-East Asian countries.
In the US there are major differences in wages received by
men and women.   Women who are over 52 per cent of the
total workforce are predominantly located in the assembly and
labour sectors, where they are over 75 per cent of the
workers and receive wages between $4 to $6 per hour, while
men largely in the technical and craft areas receive $5 to $9
per hour (Axelrad, 1979).

TABLE 7.5 *Wages for women workers (in US $) in US offshore plants (1979)*

Country	Starting wage			Wage after two years employment	Monthly expenses
	Daily basic	with bonus	Monthly wages		
Indonesia	.80	–	19.20	29.25	26.00
Philippines	1.40	1.90	34.00–45.00	75.00	37.00
Malaysia	2.00	2.25	54.00–60.00	100.00	45.00
Hong Kong	5.00	6.35	120.00–152.00	187.00	123.00

Source: Grossman, 1979, p. 10

FACTORS UNDERLYING OFFSHORE PRODUCTION

While the employment of a low-wage female assembly work-force (7) has enabled the electronics industry to rapidly develop and expand, it was particularly the lowering of pro-duction costs through the large-scale employment of a cheap female workforce in South-East Asia that led to the growth of transnational production with its offshore assembly work. This was able to develop due to a variety of factors: elec-tronic components and goods have a high value to weight ratio and thus have a relatively low transport cost, enabling easy movement between the home country and offshore assem-bly site. In addition, the government policy and legislation of many Third World developing nations frequently encourages direct foreign investment in offshore sites particularly through local incentives. And in the US the presence of tariff regu-lations 806.30 and 807.00 have enabled large-scale imports of electronic goods from offshore plants. These regulations require that producers use parts made in the US and assess duty only on the value added to the product abroad (see Chang, 1971).
    The key role that the search for low-wage labour has played in the development of transnational production with offshore assembly work is widely acknowledged by company manage-ment:
    The pay differential [in Third World countries] allows the electronics industry to remain competitive' (Lucas, quoted in Helvarg, 1978, p. 3).

of course the reason for going there is labor, down there

[in the offshore plant] we pay 45^C an hour, here it's 72^C - that's about a 33% difference right there (Van Fleet, quoted in NACLA, 1977, p. 22).

Y.S. Chang in his study of the semiconductor industry and offshore assembly found that company management ranked the low-wage rate as their main reason for locating their assembly work offshore. The availability of trainable labour was also seen as important (1971, p. 31). A range of different reasons however are given by management to justify and/or explain their exploitation of women as a cheap labour force. Corporation executives provide the following examples: (8)

'Women are much more agile and dexterous - you need agile fingers' (Philips, Manager, 1979).

'Men are not satisfactory - they make mistakes' (Allied Industries Ltd, Manager, 1979).

'It's because of the very precise nature of the work. The dexterity of the female has been found to be better than the male' (Lucas, quoted in Helvarg, 1978, p. 4).

'Women have traditionally worked in this area and have more concentration than men' (Thorn Radio Industries Ltd, Manager, 1979).

'Women are not interested in heavy lifting or dirty work. They prefer assembly. Men find it quite normal to lift and do dirty work' (Allied Industries Ltd, Manager, 1979).

The Malaysia Government brochure 'Malaysia: The Solid State for Electronics', summed up these views very aptly when it stated:

The manual dexterity of the oriental female is famous the world over. Her hands are small and she works fast with extreme care. Who therefore could be better qualified by nature and inheritance to contribute to the efficiency of a bench-assembly production line than the oriental girl...? (Federal Industrial Development Authority, 1971, quoted by Lim, 1978, p. 7).

Social and cultural stereotypes, traditions and expectations concerning the status and role of women are thus being used by corporation management to justify the large-scale targeting and exploitation of women. The learned skill of agility and dexterity is implied to be an innate quality found only in women, and the widespread acceptance and emphasis on such myths consequently enable the corporations to develop female-intensive industries (see Elson and Pearson, 1981 for a further discussion of these issues). Traditional views on the role of women in the workforce as supplementary wage-earners also enables the corporations to maintain the low wage levels they pay to women.

In contrast to the openness of discussion on how women are

such hardworking and dexterous employees in the industry as
shown in the above examples, only rarely are the low wage
levels paid to women publicly discussed by industry and company leaders as a relevant issue. The following management
comments provide such insights on the targeting of women as
a low wage assembly workforce:

'Men don't want to do assembly work as they go for higher
pay' (Thorn Radio Industries Ltd, Manager, 1979).

'The reason that large numbers of women are assemblers is
related to wages. Men can get higher wages in other jobs
- it's harder for women' (AWA Ltd, Production Manager,
1979).

'We hire girls because they have less energy, are more disciplined, and are easier to control' (Personnel Officer, Intel
Corporation, Malaysia, quoted by Grossman, 1979, p. 2).
Regardless of the justifications provided by electronic industry management, a new international division of production
and labour is emerging at a global level, which is dependent
on a low-wage labour force of predominantly women workers
in both the home country base and offshore assembly site.

THE TARGETED WORKFORCE: A PROFILE OF WOMEN WORKERS

Large numbers of women are in fact being employed under
this exploitative system. It is estimated that between
300,000 and 500,000 women are employed as assembly workers
in US electronic offshore plants in South-East Asia. (9)
And in the US itself in 1978 227,800 women were employed in
this industry - a large proportion of whom were production
workers (US Department of Labor, 1979, quoted in Snow,
1980, p. 35). Migrant women feature largely in this transnational assembly workforce. Both in the First World countries' production plants and in the Third World assembly sites.
In the US, in the Santa Clara, San Jose and Boston production areas, immigrant workers make up a large proportion of
the electronics workforce (see Axelrad, 1979; Bernstein et
al., 1977 and Snow, 1980). Snow reports in his study of
this industry that 44.8 per cent of blue collar workers in the
San Jose area in 1978 were from ethnic minorities (1980, p.
45); and that 'electronics production work has also increasingly been carried out by Third World workers, usually
women, in the US' (ibid., p. 6). The position of women in
this US workforce - particularly migrant women is succinctly
summarised by an assembly-line worker in a Santa Clara semiconductor firm when she said:

'85% of the production workers are women and 50% of those
are third world. They are promoted very slowly, although

affirmative action is helping that now.   An Hawaiian woman
is supervisor.   There is only one woman engineer in the
whole place.   And almost all the electronics technicians
are men.   So it's pretty blatant discrimination' (quoted in
Bernstein et al., 1977, p. 28)

My research in New Zealand indicates that migrant women
make up a large sector of the electronics assembly workforce
in transnational corporations.   For example in 1979 in Thorn
Radio Industries NZ Ltd, a United Kingdom company, 80 per
cent of all production workers were Polynesian women immigrants mainly from Samoa.

In the US electronics offshore plants, large numbers of
migrant women are employed in all of the South-East Asian
countries.   Studies in Hong Kong, Malaysia, Philippines,
Singapore, South Korea and Thailand all indicate that a high
percentage of the female assembly workforce in US offshore
plants are migrant women. (10)   Several factors have led to
the large involvement of migrant women in the offshore industry.   One of the key reasons is economic necessity.   In
many instances many of the women have come on their own
from rural areas in the search for employment - quite a new
migratory pattern particularly in South-East Asia, in marked
contrast to the well-documented migratory movements of men
and families.   These women have frequently migrated to the
cities, and free trade zones (a large employment area for
export-oriented offshore plants) in response to extensive
electronics company recruitment drives (Grossman, 1979, p.
10;   Heyzer, 1980 and Lim, 1978, p. 30).   The demand by
transnational electronics corporations seeking a large female
assembly workforce for their offshore plants has often been
assisted by the policies of the local governments.   For
example in Singapore the government have had extensive
housing resettlement schemes, which have resulted in the
movement of a potential workforce to closer proximity to the
offshore production sites (Lim, 1978, p. 7).

Women have also migrated from their home countries in
search of work;   this has been the case particularly in Malaysia.   Heyzer, in her study of female Malaysian migrants and
capital accumulation in Singapore, records that large numbers
of young rural women have migrated from the New Villages
and Kampongs for manufacturing work in Singapore.   She
states:

> The recruitment of foreign labour and young female labour
> in the industries of Singapore must be seen within the con-
> text of investment decisions by various multinationals to set
> up their subsidiaries in Singapore within the expansion
> phase of international business.... There was an urgent
> need for a labour force content to work for low wages in
> industries offering semi-skilled and unskilled jobs.   Re-
> cruiting agents were sent to the New Villages and Kampongs
> of West Malaysia to lure the young female engaged in subsis-

tence production with the promise of wage work, urban
living quarters and the bright light of Singapore (Heyzer,
1980, p. 2).
In these offshore assembly plants the fact that a high percentage of the workers are migrant women who are recruited
specifically for low-wage assembly work is further evidence
in studies which show that for the majority of the women this
is their first job. (11)   Generally too in most of the assembly plants in South-East Asia these women are young.   For
example Enloe reports that in the offshore electronics industry in Malaysia firms such as Hitachi, Motorola, National,
Semiconductor and Philips rely on young women for 90 per
cent of their labour force (1979, p. 7).   Thus the development of transnational production with the movement offshore
of labour-intensive assembly production, particularly into
South-East Asia, in the search for a low-wage workforce has
resulted in the migration of large numbers of women for this
work, the majority of whom are young and in their first paid
employment.   These offshore plants have also exploited the
pools of labour already available in and around the urban
areas.
    The large-scale and widespread recruitment by company
personnel of women from rural and urban areas for electronics
offshore assembly is closely related to their requirements of a
high school educated workforce (Grossman, 1979, pp. 8-10
and Lim, 1978, p. 13).   This is as much related to the
nature of the work as it is to the desire of the companies for
a 'disciplined' and 'submissive' workforce - to ensure high
productivity levels.   The offshore electronics assembly industry in South-East Asia is thus *not* providing work for the
large sectors of unemployed men and women.   It is in fact
generally drawing on a group of young, high school educated
women who have not been involved in paid employment before.
    But employment as an electronics assembly worker in an
offshore plant is at best a dubious position.   Wages are low
and possibility of job loss particularly through layoffs is
high.   For example in the 1974-5 recession '15,000 workers,
one third of all electronic workers, lost their jobs in Singapore' (New Nation, 1975, quoted in Grossman, 1979, p. 10).
Heyzer suggests that two-thirds of those who lost their jobs
were migrants, and that they were sent home to their villages
in West Malaysia (1980, p. 26).   A similar situation of job
loss was reported in the Philippines, Malaysia, South Korea,
Taiwan and Hong Kong during this period (Paglaban, 1978,
p. 18 and Grossman, 1979, p. 10).   Little, if any, positive
union or labour assistance is available to women workers in
this industry.   In the Philippines, Malaysia, Indonesia and
Hong Kong most factories, especially US corporations, have no
unions.   In Singapore, Taiwan and South Korea where unions
are encouraged by the government - they in fact are little
help to the workers as they often operate in the interests of

management through government control. (12)   The labour
conditions and regulations that apply within the factory situation in many South-East Asian plants is well described by a
US businessman in Singapore: 'If I had been assigned to
write the Singapore labour ordinances, I could not have done
a better job for my company or any other' (NACLA, 1977, p.
16).

A similar situation also confronts the predominantly female
assembly workforce in the companies' plants in the US: in the
San Jose, Santa Clara Valley area - Silicon Valley - very few
companies have union organisation.   Axelrad reports that at
most only approximately 5.6 per cent of the electronics workforce in the Santa Clara Valley is represented by unions
(1979, p. 13).   With so little union or labour assistance
available the workers are in a very vulnerable position with
few possibilities to attempt to change, in any way, their exploited work situation.

HEALTH AND SAFETY

Employment in electronics production carries with it the possibility of exposure to a range of health and safety hazards.
Many   reports of ill health and accidents have been made by
women involved in electronic assembly work in South-East
Asia.   In South Korea the union of the US electronic corporation, Control Data, reported that 34 per cent of the union
members are suffering from one disease or another - stomach
disorders, skin diseases and eye trouble (Control Data Korean
Labour Union, 1978, p. 10).   Paglaban in his extensive
study of the Philippines electronics export industry reports a
situation of widespread physical ill health and discomfort
among workers who frequently complain of acid burns, skin
rashes from epoxy resins and other 'allergic reactions' from
exposure to solvents like trichloroethylene (TCE).   Paglaban
reports workers also experiencing nausea, dizziness and lung
trouble from breathing gas fumes, probably from lead, zinc
oxide or cadmium oxide (1978).

The most common complaint is deteriorating eyesight and
frequent headaches caused through the daily use of a micro-
scope for eight hours to carry out the fine assembly work on
electronic components.   This is the case in many of the factories where particularly after two to three years' work, up to
50 per cent of the women assembly workers complain of deteriorating eyesight and headaches (Bernstein et al., 1977, pp.
32-3; NACLA, 1977, p. 17; Grossman, 1979, p. 11; Lim,
1978, and Blake and Moonstan, 1980, p. 24).

In the US home base production sites women workers also
complain of a range of physical problems and exposure to dangerous materials.   But as has also been found in the offshore
plants, the industry management is not prepared to publicly

acknowledge the hazards and risks to the workers' health as
a cause for serious concern.   However to the women themselves it is of major importance, for as Grossman points out
in her study of US offshore assembly in South-East Asia,
'most electronics workers will be forced by deteriorating
vision to leave their jobs before they are thirty' (1979, p.
15).   And the probability of finding other employment is
virtually non-existent for these women in South-East Asia.

IN CONCLUSION

The large numbers of women employed in assembly work production particularly in the offshore plants are involved in a
vulnerable and exploitative situation.   They receive very low
wages, generally have little union or labour assistance, are
often involved in job layoffs and work in a situation frequently exposed to health and safety hazards.   Corporations in
the constant search for low-wage labour have thus evolved a
system of transnational production which in conjunction with
the high technology work in their home-based sites involves
the large-scale assembly work of their goods in offshore
plants - carried out by a predominantly female workforce
large numbers of whom are young, migrant women.   As the
electronics industry is one of the key areas of growth in the
world economy (see 'Standard and Poors Industry Surveys',
1979 and US Department of Commerce, 1979), current trends
would tend to indicate that this exploitation of women, particularly as assembly workers in offshore sites, will continue
and increase as further corporations, particularly from
Europe, move into transnational production in the search for
low-wage labour.

NOTES

1   Information on this project and research to hand can be
    obtained from Dr Krishna Kumar, Impact Project, Culture
    Learning Institute, East West Center, 1777 East West Rd,
    Honolulu, Hawaii 96848.
2   Axelrad's statistics on the major employment categories
    for the Santa Clara workforce are drawn from two sources:
    1) affirmative action data from an electronics trades assoc-
    iation survey of ninety-one unnamed companies and 2)
    government survey of eight individual companies.
3   The following references provide data on the establishment
    of US offshore production plants: (Hong Kong) Chang,
    1971, p. 19;   (Indonesia) North America Congress on
    Latin America (NACLA) nr 4 April 1977, p. 15;   (Malay-
    sia) ibid., p. 13;   (Philippines) Paglaban, 1978, p. 16:
    (Singapore) NACLA, 1977, p. 13;   (South Korea) Chang,

1971, p. 19;   (Taiwan) ibid., p. 19 and (Thailand) UNCTAD, 1975, p. 17.

4   The list of the 194 electronics assembly plants operating offshore in South-East Asian countries in 1976 can be obtained from: North American Congress on Latin America, P O Box 57, Cathedral Station, New York, NY 10025.

5   In the New Zealand electronics industry a very similar sexual division of labour has emerged.   Men predominate in the professional, technical area (95.52 per cent), in the administrative and managerial group (97.37 per cent) and in the sales sector (91.74 per cent).   Women on the other hand are employed primarily in the clerical sector (78.44 per cent) and assembly area (71.73 per cent) (Hancock, 1980, p. 4).

6   The New Zealand electronics industry - particularly the dominant consumer industry, provides an example of a further extension of this process.   It is dependent on the high technology of the USA, Japan and Europe and on the basis of the application of this technology, New Zealand imports electronic materials, components and products.   These imported goods have been manufactured in overseas labour intensive semi-skilled production sites - generally by a predominantly female workforce.   The imported goods are then finally assembled into products for the New Zealand market by an assembly workforce that is also predominantly female (Hancock, 1980).

7   A similar situation is found in New Zealand where in the electronics industry women received 22.74 per cent less than men per hour.   The average ordinary rate per hour (1979) for men was $4.22 (NZ) while women received $3.26 (NZ) per hour.   An example of the low wages women are paid in this industry is shown in the following chart:

Production and related workers: wages (NZ$) per 40 hours

Position	Wage	Proportion of women	Proportion of men
Assembly	$122	88%	12%
Quality control	125	60%	40%
Workshop	190	0	100%
Technician	180	33%	67%
Supervisor	210	0	100%

Source: Hancock, 1980, pp. 12-14.

8   The following management quotations unless stated otherwise come from interviews with executives in transnational

    electronics corporations operating in New Zealand.
    Interviews were carried out by the author from August
    to October 1979.

9   NACLA (1977, p. 15) estimates that at least 500,000
    women are involved, while Grossman (1979, p. 3) gives a
    figure of 200,000 to 300,000.

10 This data is part of preliminary material gathered in
    South-East Asia by the Women and Transnational Corpora-
    tions project, see note 1.

11 Von de Mehden in 'Industrial Policy in Malaysia' found
    that two-thirds of the women workers in the Bayan Lepas
    Free Trade Zone were new entrants to the labour force.
    Reported in Lim (1978) p. 30.

12 For a discussion of the offshore electronics industry and
    unionisation see NACLA, 1977, p. 16.

Bibliography

Abadan-Unat, N. (1977), Implications of migration on emanci-
pation and pseudo-emancipation of Turkish women, 'Inter-
national Migration Review', vol. XI, no. 1, pp. 31-57.
Alexander, S. (1976), Women's work in nineteenth-century
London: A study of the years 1820-50, in A. Oakley and
J. Mitchell (eds), 'The Rights and Wrongs of Women', Har-
mondsworth, Penguin, pp. 59-111.
Allen, S. (1971), 'New Minorities, Old Conflicts: Asian and
West Indian Migrants in Britain', New York, Random House.
Allen, S. (1979), A triple burden, paper presented at the
Women's Anthropology Group Seminar, The Transnational
Institute, Amsterdam, December.
Allen, S. (1980), Perhaps a seventh person?, 'Women's
Studies International Quarterly', vol. 3, no. 4, pp. 325-38.
Allen, S. et al. (1977), 'Work, Race and Immigration', Univer-
sity of Bradford.
American Electronics Association (1978), 'Benchmark Wage and
Salary Survey', Fall.
Andezian, S. and Streiff, J. (1981), Les réseaux sociaux des
femmes maghrebines immigrées en Provence-Cote d'Azur,
unpublished thesis, Thèse de doctorat de 3ème cycle,
Université de Nice.
Anthias, F. and Ayres, R. (1979), Constitutional struggle in
Cypriot left politics, paper presented to BSA Conference,
Aberystwyth, 1979.
Anwar, M. (1979), 'The Myth of Return', London, Heinemann.
Arizpe, L. (1980), Women in agrarian societies and rural out-
migration, paper presented at the meeting on research on
the Status of Women, Development and Population Trends:
Evaluation and Prospects UNESCO, Paris, 25-28 November
(SS-80/Conf.627/col.33).
Arondo, M. (1975), 'Moi la Bonne', Paris, Stock.
Axelrad, M. and PHASE staff (1979), Profile of the electronics
industry workforce in the Santa Clara Valley, PHASE.
Barker, D. and Allen, S. (eds) (1976), 'Dependence and Ex-
ploitation in Work and Marriage', London, Longmans.
Barker, D. and Allen, S. (eds) (1976a), 'Sexual Divisions and
Society: Process and Change', London, Tavistock.
Barrett, M. (1980), 'Women's Oppression Today', London,
Verso and NLB.
Barron, R.D. and Norris, G.M. (1976), Sexual divisions and
the dual labour market, in D. Barker and S. Allen (eds),

'Sexual Divisions in Society: Process and Change', London, Tavistock.

Baudouin, T., Collin, M. and Guillerm, D. (1978), Women and immigrants: marginal workers?, in C. Crouch and A. Pezzorno (eds), 'The Resurgence of Class Conflict in Western Europe since 1968, Volume 2, Comparative Analysis', London, Macmillan.

Baumgartner-Karabak, A. and Landesberger, G. (1978), 'Die Verkauften Bräuter', Reinbek bei Hamburg, Rowolt.

Bayliss, F.J. and Coates, J.B. (1965), West Indians at work in Nottingham, 'Race', vol. 7, no. 2, October, pp. 157-66.

Beechey, V. (1978), Women and production: a critical analysis of some sociological theories of women's work, in A. Kuhn and A.M. Wolpe (eds), 'Feminism and Materialism', London, Routledge & Kegan Paul.

BELC (1976), Les femmes immigrées et la formation, 'Migrants-Formation', no. 14-15, March.

Bellini, J. (1974/5), European migrant labour: Present and future conditional, 'New Community', vol. IV, no. 1, pp. 5-18.

Berger, J. and Mohr, J. (1975), 'The Seventh Man', Harmondsworth, Penguin.

Bernstein, A. et al. (1977), 'Silicon Valley: Paradise or Paradox?', Pacific Studies Center, October.

Billiet, A. et al. (1974), 'Tentative d'approche de la situation de la femmes immigrée', Bruxelles, Service Social des Etrangers.

Blake, M.L. and Moonstan, C. (1980), Women in transnational corporations: The electronics industry in Thailand, Report for the project on Women and Transnational Corporations, East West Center, Honolulu, Hawaii.

Bonacich, E. (1980), Class approaches to ethnicity and race, 'The Insurgent Sociologist', vol. X, no. 2, pp. 9-23.

Bonacich, E. and Modell, J. (1980), 'The Economic Basis of Ethnic Solidarity: Small Business in the Japanese American Community', London, University of California Press.

Bosanquet, N. and Doeringer, P.B. (1973), Is there a dual labour market in Great Britain?, 'Economic Journal', vol. 83, pp. 421-35.

Brooks, D. and Singh, K. (1979), 'Aspirations versus Opportunities: Asian and White School-leavers in the West Midlands', London, Commission for Racial Equality.

Browning, H. and Feindt, W. (1971), Patterns of migration to Monterey, Mexico, 'International Migration Review', vol. 5, no. 3, pp. 309-24.

Bruegel, I. (1979), Women as a reserve army of labour: a note on recent British experience, 'Feminist Review', no. 3, pp. 12-23.

Bundesanstalt für Arbeit (1980), Sonderdruck Socialversicherungspflichtig beschaftigte Arbeitnehmer Ende Juni 1979, Nurnberg.

'Business Times' (1977), Singapore's electronics industry need for more skilled workers, Singapore, 21 November.

Burawoy, M. (1980), Migrant labour in South Africa and the United States, in T. Nicholls (ed.) 'Capital and Labour', London, Athlone Press.

Castells, M. (1975), Immigrant workers and class struggles in advanced capitalism: the Western European experience, 'Politics and Society', vol. 5, no. 1, pp. 33-66.

Castles, S. (1980a), Structural racism: ethnic minorities in Western Europe, 'PCR Information', World Council of Churches, Geneva, no. 8, pp. 18-40.

Castles, S. (1980b), The social time-bomb: education of an underclass in West Germany, 'Race and Class', vol. XXI, no. 4, pp. 369-88.

Castles, S. and Kosack, G. (1973), 'Immigrant Workers and the Class Structure', London, Oxford University Press and the Institute of Race Relations.

Castles, S. and Kosack, G. (1974), How the trade unions try to control and integrate immigrant workers, 'Race', vol. 15, no. 4, pp. 497-514.

Central Bureau of Statistics (1981), The Hague, Netherlands.

Chang, Y.S. (1971), 'The Transfer of Technology: Economics of offshore Assembly; the Case of the Semiconductor Industry', UNITAR.

Cheetham, J. (1972), 'Social Work with Immigrants', London, Routledge & Kegan Paul.

Churches' Committee on Migrant Workers (CCMW) (1974), 'Women Migrants', Geneva, World Council of Churches.

Churches' Committee on Migrant Workers (1978), 'Migrant Women Speak', London, Search Press.

Cirba, L. and Costa-Lascoux, J. (1980), Les femmes immigrées: du role traditionnel au travail salarie, paper presented at the Conference of the Société Française de Sociologie, Nantes, 6-7 June.

Cohen, L. (1977), The female factor in development, 'Society', September/October, pp. 27-30.

Cohen, R. (1981), The end to the migrant labour boom, 'Newsletter of International Labour Studies', no. 10, April.

Commission for Racial Equality (1978), 'Between Two Cultures', 2nd ed., London, Commission for Racial Equality.

Commission for Racial Equality (1979), 'Ethnic Minorities in Britain', London, CRE.

Costa-Lascoux, J. (1980), Une legislation pour une nouvelle politique de l'immigration?, 'Pluriel', no. 22, pp. 7-31.

Coyle, A. (1982), Sex and skill in the organisation of the clothing industry, in J. West, 'Work, Women and the Labour Market', London, Routledge & Kegan Paul.

Crine, S. (1979), 'The Hidden Army', London, Low Pay Unit.

Davison, B. (1968), No place back home: a study of Jamaicans returning to Kingston, Jamaica, 'Race', vol. 9, no. 4, April, pp. 499-509.

Deakin, N. (1970), 'Colour Citizenship and British Society', London, Panther.

Delcourt, J. (1975), 'The Housing of Migrant Workers: A Case of Social Improvidence?', Brussels, Commission of the European Communities.

Department of Employment (1975), Unemployment among workers from racial minority groups, 'Employment Gazette', vol. 83, no. 9, pp. 868-71.

Department of Employment (1976), 'The Role of Immigrants in the Labour Market', London, Department of Employment, Unit for Manpower Services.

Dex, S. (1978), Measuring women's unemployment, 'Social and Economic Administration', vol. 12, no. 2, pp. 136-41.

Dex, S. (1979), Economists' theories of the economics of discrimination, 'Ethnic and Racial Studies', vol. 2, no. 1, pp. 90-108.

Dex, S. (1979a), A note on discrimination in employment and its effects on black youths, 'Journal of Social Policy', vol. 8, part 3, pp. 357-69.

Dex, S. (1981), School-leavers' prospects, Department of Employment Research Papers Series.

Driver, G. (1980), 'Beyond Underachievement', London, Commission for Racial Equality.

du Boulay, J. (1974), 'Portrait of a Greek Mountain Village', Oxford, Clarendon Press.

Dummett, A. (1976), 'Citizenship and Nationality', London, Runnymede Trust.

Edholm, F., Harris, O. and Young, K. (1977), Conceptualising women, 'Critique of Anthropology', vol. 3, 9 and 10, pp. 101-30.

Eisner, G. (1961), 'Jamaica 1830-1930: A Study in Economic Growth', Manchester University Press.

Elson, D. and Pearson, R. (1981), The subordination of women and the internationalisation of factory production, in Young, K. et al. (eds), 'Of Marriage and the Market', London, CSE Books.

Engelbrektsson, U. (1978), The force of tradition: Turkish migrants at home and abroad, 'Gothenburg Studies in Social Anthropology', 1, Acta Universitatis Gothoburgensis.

Enloe, C.H. (1979), Profile Malaysia: On the way to 1990, 'Asian Thought and Society'.

Freeman, C. (1982), The 'understanding' employer, in J. West (ed.), 'Work, Women and the Labour Market', London, Routledge & Kegan Paul.

Fonda, N. and Moss, P. (eds) (1976), 'Mothers in Employment', Brunel University Management Programme/Thomas Coram Research Unit.

Foner, N. (1975), Women, work and migration: Jamaicans in London, 'Urban Anthropology', vol. 4, no. 3, Fall, pp. 229-49.

Foner, N. (1979), 'Jamaica Farewell', London, Routledge & Kegan Paul.

Genovese, E.D. (1971), 'In Red and Black: Marxian Explora-
tion into Southern and Afro-American History', New York,
Vintage Books.

Girvan, N. (1972), 'Foreign Capital and Economic Underdevelopment in Jamaica', Kingston, Institute of Social and Economic Research, University of the West Indies.

Granotier, B. (1971 and 1979), 'Les Travailleurs Immigrés',
Paris, Maspero.

Gregory, E. (1969), Childminding in Paddington, in 'The
Medical Officer', vol. 122, no. 10, 5 September.

Grossman, R. (1979), Women's place in the integrated circuit,
'South-east Asia Chronicle', no. 66, January/February and
'Pacific Research', vol. 9, no. 5-6, July/October, pp. 2-17.

Hakim, C. (1978), Sexual divisions within the labour force:
occupational segregation, 'Department of Employment
Gazette', November, pp. 1264-8.

Hall, S. et al. (1978), 'Policing the Crisis', London, Macmillan.

Hancock, M. (1980), 'The Electronics Industry in New Zealand:
Exploitation of Women Workers and International Dependence',
Working Paper Series, Culture Learning Institute, East West
Center, Honolulu.

Haringey Area Management Team (1981), 'West Green Child
Care Survey, Summary', London, Haringey Council.

Haringey Employment Project (1980), 'The Clothing Industry in the Cypriot Community', Draft Report, London,
Haringey Council.

Held, T. and Levy, R. (eds) (1976), 'Femme, Famille et
Société', Vevey, Delta.

Helvarg, D. (1978), Corporate aliens flood Baja, 'San Diego
Newsline', vol. 2, issue 12, 20-25 December.

Hess-Buechler, V. (1976), Something funny happened on the
way to the Agora; a comparison of Bolivian and Spanish
Galician female migrants, 'Anthropological Quarterly', vol.
49, pp. 62-7 and Introduction.

Hewitt, P. (1976), Women's rights in law and practice, 'New
Community', vol. v, no. 1-2.

Heyzer, N. (1980), From rural subsistence to an industrial
peripheral workforce: An examination of female Malaysian
migrants and capital accumulation in Singapore, final draft
of paper to be published by the International Labour
Organisation, Geneva.

Hoel, B. (1982), Contemporary clothing 'sweatshops', Asian
female labour and collective organisation, in J. West (ed.),
'Work, Women and the Labour Market', London, Routledge &
Kegan Paul.

Hoffman-Nowotny, H.J. (1977), Sociological and demographic
aspects of the changing status of migrant women in Europe,
'Zeitschrift fur Bevölkerungswissenschaft', Heft 2, pp. 3-22.

Hommes et Migrations (1971), 'Alphabetisation et promotion
feminine', Documents 805, Paris.

Hood, C. et al. (1970), 'The Children of West Indian Immigrants', London, Institute of Race Relations.

Hope, E. et al. (1976), Homeworkers in North London, in D.L. Barker and S. Allen (eds), 'Dependence and Exploitation in Work and Marriage', London, Longman.

Hubbuck, J. and Carter, S. (1981), 'Half a Chance? A Report on Job Discrimination against Young Blacks in Nottingham', London, Commission for Racial Equality and Nottingham and District Community Relations Council.

Humphries, J. (1977), Class struggle and the persistence of the working-class family, in 'Cambridge Journal of Economics', vol. 1, pp. 241-58.

Institute of Race Relations (1979), 'Police Against Black People', Race and Class Pamphlet, no. 6, London, IRR.

James, A.G. (1974), 'Sikh Children in Britain', London, Oxford University Press and Institute of Race Relations.

Kamenko, V. (1978), 'Unter uns War Krieg, Autobiografie einer jugoslawischen arbeiterin', Berlin, Rotbuch Verlag.

Kellner, P. (1981), Maggie's missing million, 'New Statesman', Friday 27 March.

Kiray, M. (1976), The family of the immigrant worker, in N. Abadan-Unat (ed.), 'Turkish Workers in Europe, 1969-75', Leiden, E.J. Brill.

Kosack, G. (1976), Migrant women: the move to Western Europe - a step towards emancipation?, 'Race and Class', vol. 17, no. 4, pp. 370-9.

Kudat, A. and Sabuncuoglu, M. (1980), The changing composition of Europe's guestworker population, 'Monthly Labour Review', vol. 103, no. 10, October, pp. 10-17.

'Labour Supply and Migration in Europe' (Economic Survey of Europe: Part II) (1979), Geneva, ECE and United Nations.

Lacoste-Dujardin, C. (1976), 'Dialogue des Femmes eu Ethnologie', Paris, Maspero.

Ladman, J. (1977), Economic impact of the Mexican border industrialisation program: Agua Prieta Sonora, Center for Latin American Studies, Arizona State University.

Land, H. (1980), The Family Wage, 'Feminist Review', no. 6, pp. 55-77.

Lawrence, D. (1974), 'Black Migrants: White Natives', London, Cambridge University Press.

Lebon, A. (1979), Feminisation de la main d'oeuvre entrangère, 'Hommes et Migrations', no. 963, February, pp. 27-33.

Leeds, A. (1976), Women in the migratory process: a reductionist outlook, 'Anthropological Quarterly', vol. 49, pp. 69-76.

Leonetti, I. and Levi, F. (1979), 'Femmes et Immigrées', Paris, Documentation Française.

Levi, F. (1977), Modèles et pratiques en changement, 'Ethnologie Francaise', vol. 7, no. 3, pp. 287-98.

Ley, K. (1979), 'Frauen in der Emigration: Eine soziologische Untersuchung des Lebens und Arbeitssituation italienischer Frauen in der Schweiz', Frauenfeld und Stuttgart, Huber Verlag.

Lim, L.Y.C. (1978), 'Women Workers in Multinational Corporations: The Case of the Electronics Industry in Malaysia and Singapore', Michigan Occasional Paper, IX, Fall.

Lomas, G. (1975), Race and employment, 'New Society', 15 May.

Louden, D. (1978), Self-esteem and locus of control: Some findings on immigrant adolescents in Britain, 'New Community', vol. VI, no. 3, pp. 218-34.

Lozells Social Development Centre (1975), 'Wednesday's Children: A Report on Under-Fives' Provision in Handsworth', Birmingham, Commission for Racial Equality.

Macek, O. and Mayer, B. (1972), From a study on mental hygiene and social problems of Yugoslav workers in an Austrian textile factory, in P. Verhaegen (ed.), 'Mental Health in Foreign Workers', Louvain, ACCO.

MacDonald, J.S. and MacDonald, L.B. (1972), 'The Invisible Immigrants', London, Runnymede Trust.

Maher, V. (1981), Work, consumption and authority within the household: A Moroccan case, in K. Young et al. (eds), 'Of Marriage and the Market', London, CSE Books.

Majava, A. (1974), 'Family Problems of Finnish Emigrants', reply to the IUFO questionnaire (pro manuscripto).

Mayhew, K. and Rosewell, B. (1978), Immigrants and occupational crowding in Great Britain, 'Oxford Bulletin of Economics and Statistics', vol. 40, no. 3, August, pp. 223-48.

Meillassoux, C. (1981), 'Maidens, Meal and Money', Cambridge University Press.

Mernissi, F. (1975), 'Beyond the Veil: Male Female Dynamics in a Modern Muslim Society', London, Wiley & Sons.

Migrants' Action Group (1981), Triple oppression - and now repatriation, MAG, 68 Chalton St, London N W 1.

Miles, R. (1982), 'Racism and Migrant Labour', London, Routledge & Kegan Paul.

Miles, R. and Phizacklea, A. (1977), 'The T.U.C., Black Workers and New Commonwealth Immigration, 1954-1973', Research Unit on Ethnic Relations Working Papers, no. 6, University of Aston.

Miles, R. and Phizacklea, A. (1978), The T.U.C. and black workers, 1974-76, 'British Journal of Industrial Relations', vol. XVI, no. 2, pp. 195-207.

Miles, R. and Phizacklea, A. (1979), Some introductory observations on race and politics in Britain, in R. Miles and A. Phizacklea (eds), 'Racism and Political Action in Britain', London, Routledge & Kegan Paul.

Minces, J. (1973), 'Les travailleurs etrangers en France', Paris, Seuil.

Moore, J. (1971), Mexican Americans and cities: A study of migration and use of formal resources, 'International Migration Review', vol. 5, no. 3, pp. 292-308.

Moore, R. and Wallace, T. (1975), 'Slamming the Door', London, Martin Robertson.

Morokvasic, M. (1974), Les femmes immigrées au travail, paper presented at the CEE Conference on Migration Problems, Louvain-la-Neuve, February, mimeo.

Morokvasic, M. (1975), L'immigration feminine en France: Etat de la question, 'Année Sociologique', vol. 26, pp. 563-75.

Morokvasic, M. (1980), Yugoslav women in France, Germany and Sweden, study report, Centre Nationale de la Recherche Scientifique, Paris.

Morokvasic, M. (forthcoming), 'A Fourfold Oppression?'

Münscher, A. (1980), 'Ausländische Frauen, Annotierte bibliographie', Munchen, Deutsches Jugendinstitut.

Nikolinakos, N. (1975), Draft of a general theory of migration in late capitalism, 'Proceedings of International Conference on Migrant Workers', International Institute for Comparative Social Studies of the Science Centre, Berlin.

North American Congress on Latin America (NACLA) (1977), Electronics: The global industry, 'Latin America and Empire Report', vol. IX, no. 4, April.

Oakley, R. (1979), Family, kinship and patronage, in V. Saifullah Khan (ed.), 'Minority Families in Britain', London, Macmillan.

Organisation of Economic Co-operation and Development (1974-80), 'SOPEMI', Paris, OECD.

Paglaban, E. (1978), Philippines: Workers in the export industry, 'Pacific Research', vol. IX, no. 3 and 4, March-June 1978.

Palmer, I. (1979), Continuing subordination of women in the development process, 'Special Issue of Institute of Development Studies Bulletin', April, vol. 10, no. 3.

Peach, C. (1978/9), British unemployment cycles and West Indian immigration, 1955-1974, 'New Community', vol. VII, no. I, pp. 40-2.

Phillips, A. and Taylor, B. (1980), Sex and skill: notes towards a feminist economics, 'Feminist Review', no. 6, pp. 79-88.

Philpott, S.B. (1977), The Montserratians: Migration dependency and maintenance of island ties in England, in J.L. Watson (ed.), 'Between Two Cultures', Oxford, Blackwell.

Phizacklea, A. (1982), Migrant women and wage labour: The case of West Indian women in Britain, in J. West (ed.), 'Work, Women and the Labour Market', London, Routledge & Kegan Paul.

Phizacklea, A. and Miles, R. (1978), The strike at Grunwick, 'New Community', vol. IV, no. 3, pp. 268-78.

Phizacklea, A. and Miles, R. (1980), 'Labour and Racism', London, Routledge & Kegan Paul.

Pollack, M. (1972), 'Today's Three-Year-Olds in London', London, Heinemann Educational Books.

Portes, A. (1978), Toward a structural analysis of illegal (undocumented) immigration, 'International Migration Review', vol. 12, Winter, pp. 469-84.

Price, D. (1971), Rural to urban migration of Mexican Americans, Negroes and Angloes, 'International Migration Review', vol. 5, no. 3, pp. 281-91.

Pryce, K. (1978), Lifestyles of West Indians in Britain: A study of Bristol, 'New Community', vol. VI, no. 3, pp. 207-17.

Rampton Report (1981), 'West Indian Children in our Schools', Cmnd 8273, London, HMSO.

Redford, A. (1976), 'Labour Migration in England, 1800-1850', Manchester University Press (3rd ed.).

Rees, T. and O'Muircheartaigh, C. (1975/6), Migrant immigrant labour in Great Britain, France, West Germany, 'New Community', vol. IV, no. 4, pp. 493-500.

Rex, J. (1973), 'Race, Colonialism and the City', London, Routledge & Kegan Paul.

Rex, J. and Moore, R. (1967), 'Race, Community and Conflict', London, Oxford University Press.

Rex, J. and Tomlinson, S. (1979), 'Colonial Immigrants in a British City', London, Routledge & Kegan Paul.

Robinson, V. (1980), Correlates of Asian immigration: 1959-1974, 'New Community', vol. VIII, nos 1 and 2, pp. 115-22.

Rogers, S.C. (1976), discussion at American Anthropological Association 75th Annual Meeting, Washington DC, November.

Rose, E.J.B. et al. (1969), 'Colour and Citizenship', London, Oxford University Press.

Rubin, G. (1975), The traffic in women: notes on the 'political economy' of sex, in R. Reiter (ed.), 'Towards an Anthropology of Women', New York, Monthly Review Press.

Saifullah-Khan, V. (1974), Pakistani villagers in a British city, PhD thesis, University of Bradford.

Saifullah-Khan, V. (1976), Purdah in the British situation, in D. Leonard-Barker and S. Allen (eds), 'Dependence and Exploitation in Work and Marriage', London, Longmans.

Saifullah-Khan, V. (1979), Work and network, in S. Wallman (ed.), 'Ethnicity at Work', London, Macmillan.

Saint-Cassia, P. (1981), Patterns of politics and kinship in a Greek-Cypriot community 1920-1980, Cambridge University PhD thesis, July.

Samman, M.L. (1977), Immigration etrangère a pris un caractère plus familial, 'Economie et Statistique', no. 92, pp. 55-63.

Sanchez, C. (1978), Electronics: A dynamic export industry in the Philippines, speech delivered for ENES-ASIA, Singapore.

Sandis, E. (1971), Characteristics of Puerto Rican migrants to and from the United States, 'International Migration Review', vol. 4, no. 2, pp. 22-42.

Sayad, A. (1977), Les trois 'âges' de l'emigration algerienne, 'Actes de la Recherche en Sciences Sociale', no. 15, June, pp. 59-82.

Sciberras, E. (1977), 'Multinational Electronics Companies and National Economic Policies', Connecticutt, JAI Press.

Sharma, U. (1971), 'Rampal and his Family', London, Collins.
Sillitoe, K.K. (1972), 'West Indian School Leavers', Social Survey Division, Office of Population, Censuses and Surveys.
Singer-Kerel, J. (1980), Foreign labour and the economic crisis: the case of France, paper delivered to the ESF Conference: Cultural identity and marginalisation of migrant workers. Akademic Klausenhof 4123 Hamminkeln/uber wessel, 10-12 December.
Smith, D.J. (1977), 'Racial Disadvantage in Britain: the PEP Report', Harmondsworth, Penguin.
Smith, D.J. (1980), Unemployment and racial minority groups, 'Employment Gazette', vol. 88, no. 6, pp. 602-6.
Smith, E. (1980), The Portuguese female immigrant: The marginal man, 'International Migration Review', vol. 14, no. 1, pp. 77-92.
Snow, R. (1979), U.S. direct investment in the electronics industry by parent companies, project paper, Culture Learning Institute, East West Center, Honolulu, Hawaii, February.
Snow, R. (1980), 'The New International Division of Labour and the U.S. Workforce: The Case of the Electronics Industry', Working Paper Series, Culture Learning Institute, East West Center, Honolulu, Hawaii.
SOPEMI (1980), 'Continuous Reporting System on Migration', Paris, Organisation for Economic Co-operation and Development.
'Spare Rib' (1973), Women, blacks and the unions: Asians in Southall, no. 17, October.
Standard and Poors Corporation (1979), Electronics - electrical current analysis, 'Standard and Poors Industry Surveys', vol. 146, November.
Stolcke, V. (1981), Women's labours: The naturalisation of social inequality and women's subordination, in K. Young, C. Wolkowitz and R. McCullagh (eds), 'Of Marriage and the Market', London, CSE Books.
Surridge, B.J. (1930), 'A Survey of Rural Life in Cyprus', Cyprus, Nicosia.
Taravella, L. (1980), 'Les femmes immigrées, bibliographie annottée', Paris, CIEMM.
Thadani, V. and Todaro, M. (1978), 'Towards a Theory of Female Migration in Developing Countries', the Population Council, Centre for Policy Studies Working Paper, May, mimeo.
Tomlinson, S. (1978), West Indian children and ESN schooling, 'New Community', vol. 6, no. 3, pp. 235-42.
Uberoi, N. (1964), Sikh Women in Southall, 'Race', vol. 6, no. 1, pp. 34-40.
UNCTAD (1975), International subcontracting arrangements in electronics between developed market-economy countries and developing countries, TD/B/C2/144, Supplement, New York, United Nations.

United States Department of Commerce (1979), 'A Report on the U.S. Semiconductor Industry', Washington, DC, Department of Commerce, Industry and Trade Administration.

United States Department of Labor (1979), 'Employment and Earnings United States 1909-1978', Washington, DC, Bureau of Labor Statistics.

United States Equal Opportunity Commission (1975), 'Equal Employment Opportunity Report - 1973: Job Patterns for Minorities and Women in Private Industry', Washington, DC, USEEOC.

United States Tariff Commission (1970), Economic factors affecting the use of items 807.00 and 806.30 of the Tariff Schedules of the United States, US Government Printing Office, Washington, DC, tCi, 2Ec7.

Valabregue, C. (1973), 'L'Homme Déraciné', Paris, Mercure de France.

Van Mannen, B. (1979), 'Vrouwen te Gast', Amsterdam, Feministische Uitgeverij SARA.

Wallman, S. (ed.) (1979), 'Ethnicity at Work', London, Macmillan.

West, J. (1982), New technology and women's office work, in J. West (ed.), 'Work, Women and the Labour Market', London, Routledge & Kegan Paul.

Wilson, A. (1978), 'Finding a Voice: Asian Women in Britain', London, Virago.

Wisnewski, J. (1979), L'immigration: une problème de société, 'Hommes et Migrations - Documents', 961-2, 1 and 15 January.

World Council of Churches (1980), 'Migrant Workers and Racism in Europe', Dossier no. 7, Geneva, World Council of Churches.

Young, K. (1980), Sex specificity in migration: A case from Mexico, revised version in L. Beneria (ed.), 'Women and Development: Sexual Division of Labour in Rural Societies', New York, Praeger (1982).

Zahraoui, A. (1976), 'Les Travailleurs Algeriens en France', Paris, Maspero.

Index